CONCILIUM

Religion in the Seventies

CONCILIUM

Editorial Directors

Concilium 126 (6/1979): Project X

CHINA AS A CHALLENGE TO THE CHURCH

Edited by
Claude Geffré
and
Joseph Spae

THE SEABURY PRESS / NEW YORK

1979
The Seabury Press, 815 Second Avenue, New York, N.Y. 10017
ISBN: 0-8164-2234-6 (pbk.)   0-8164-0432-1

T. & T. Clark Ltd., 36 George Street, Edinburgh EH2 2LQ
ISBN: 0-567-30006-4 (pbk.)

Library of Congress Catalog Card Number: 79-65697
Printed in the United States of America

CONTENTS

Editorial

THE Christian conscience cannot help being stirred by the reality of new China at this end of the second millennium, if only because it counts some 900,000,000 people, the largest nation on earth. There is already a whole theological literature which attempts to grapple with the questions which the mere existence of China poses to the Church. The conferences held at Båstad and Louvain in 1974 marked an important stage, but we thought that the time had come to assess what the state of research is at present and to open up certain ways of looking at things.

China will never cease to astonish us. Since Mao Tse-tung's death, the speed of change has made us revise many precipitate judgments that served as the basis for theological elaborations which we can now see were very fragile. This very review is exposed to the same risk on account of the delays that occur between initial planning and publication. It applies, for instance, to the importance given to Maoism at a time when the powers that be in Peking have allowed ideological considerations to be overtaken by the fascination for the capitalist mode of development.

The communist revolution is, however, more than a quarter of a century old, so that we can no longer dream of a return to the China of tradition. We should in any case recall that China's resistance to Christianity goes back a long way before 1949. We draw attention to this fact in this issue. But it is not fanciful to think that the way things are developing in Chinese society could be conducive to a rapprochement with Christianity. Chinese religious life, decisively shaped as it has been by Taoism, Buddhism and Confucianism, has always been characterised by a sense of transcendence. And any form of religion has been combated implacably by Chinese communism. That, however, is because religion has meant escapism. But, as the Chinese ambassador in Belgium said recently to a group of university professors in Louvain, the fight against religion could be discontinued if religion (and especially Christianity) could prove that it is working effectively for the good of the Chinese people.

We have wanted to avoid two extremes in this issue. On the one hand, we have been wary of the rather naïve enthusiasm which led some theologians to interpret the destiny of the new China as the historical realisation of the kingdom of God. 'Service of the people' does, of course, have religious overtones and Maoism can well be seen as the most gigantic effort ever made to bring about the *new being* of individual and collective man. But God alone searches the hearts. . . . And since the death of Mao enough evidence has been piling up to make us want to ask serious questions about the degree of personal liberty and spontaneity with which the Chinese work together to build the new social being. Without going so far as to talk with Solzhenitsyn of the greatest gulag in history, we have some reason to be careful before pronouncing on the implicitly Christian values of Chinese society.

On the other hand, it would be too easy to rely upon a categorical condemnation of the Chinese revolution to relieve oneself of the task of heeding the radical question that China poses to the Church. People always talk about the otherness of China and of its imperviousness to Christianity as if these were historically fated facts. But a mere list of the historical, political and cultural causes would be insufficient if it left out the yawning gap between the historical face of the Church and the ideal of the new humanity constituted by the actual practice of the Gospel. China has always thrown out this challenge to Christians of the west to live through the constraints of life in society as well as it does itself. Maoist and post-Maoist China continue to present this challenge to all countries that call themselves Christian. One of the main things Christians have to reflect on—a process to which this issue would like to contribute—is the confrontation of the ideal of moral transcendence embodied in the new Chinese man with the ideal implied in the new Christian existence. For all its grave defects, the project of the Chinese revolution (which must not be confused with Maoism) can be thought of as a prophetic judgment on a certain form of historical Christianity and on its claim to be universal.

It is in fact this idea of a *mutual challenge* which has governed the organisation of this issue. On the one hand, China challenges the Church in its practical quest for a new humanity. On the other hand, the new freedom of man to which the Church ought to bear witness challenges the largest nation on earth. Only the future will tell whether the new being of man which is unfolding in China will be able to come to its full maturity on account of the obscure growth of the Christian seed.

The first series of four articles, then, attempts to rehearse once again the immemorial reality of China, especially in its religious and ethical dimension, and it asks in particular about the religious implications of Maoism. The remaining articles seek to decide how far today's and yesterday's China call for a reinterpretation of western Christianity. The theological themes of *transcendence* and *liberation* are given special treatment.

What these studies seek to show in their various ways is that the meeting of China and Christianity stimulates us to rethink those areas of theology that are of critical importance for our understanding of what

Christianity is about. This is particularly the case in regard to the relationship between Christianity and culture, to Christianity's claim to be universal, and to our new understanding of the Church's mission.

CLAUDE GEFFRÉ
JOSEPH SPAE

Yu-Ming Shaw

Chinese Culture in the Mind of the West

I

THE Western admirers of Chinese culture have been numerous ever since the days of Marco Polo. As is well known, the Jesuits were the first group of Westerners to conduct a systematic examination of Chinese culture. From the late sixteenth to the eighteenth century, they became the major transmitters of cultures between China and the West. To China, besides Christianity, the Jesuits exported Western sciences and some technological inventions; to the West, they introduced Chinese culture through their publications and translations of Chinese classics. For our purpose, we shall restrict our discussion of the Jesuit effort in China to their cultural and religious activities.

The essential problem that confronted the Jesuits in their work of proselytisation was how to make Christianity intelligible and attractive to the Chinese, a people who not only had many religions of their own but also a well-developed spiritual system in the form of Neo-Confucianism. The Jesuits' strategy can be summarised as containing the following. First, since they knew that Chinese scholar-officials held sway over the general populace, they decided to concentrate their work first on this special social class. Second, in order to win over this class, they engaged in serious study of Chinese classics and Chinese culture to become the intellectual equals of the Chinese literati. Third, for both religious and practical considerations, they joined the Chinese literati—almost all of whom were followers of Confucianism—in despising other Chinese religions, such as Buddhism and Taoism. Fourth, the Jesuits found that the Neo-Confucianism of the day had incorporated too many Buddhist and

1

Taoist influences and that ancient Confucianism (i.e., Confucianism before or up to the time of Confucius) contained many religious notions that were compatible with Christianity. So they decided to accept ancient Confucianism as the basis for developing a spiritual dialogue with the Chinese literati.[1] Before we discuss this last point, we should emphasise that the adoption of the above strategy should not be considered as motivated only by expediency or opportunism; it grew out of both genuine religious convictions and practical considerations.[2]

To convince the Chinese literati of the compatibility between Christianity and ancient Confucianism the Jesuit theoretical formulation contained several essential points. One, the Chinese concepts of *Shang-ti* (Lord-on-High) and *T'ien* (Heaven) as mentioned in ancient Confucian classics were equivalent to the Christian *Deus*, whereas *t'ai-chi* (Supreme Ultimate) in Neo-Confucianism was only a materialistic principle and not the guardian of the universe. Two, in ancient China the belief in the immortality of the human soul and the concept of heaven and hell had already existed. Three, Confucianism after the Han dynasty (i.e., after the third century B.C.), including Neo-Confucianism, had been a corruption of ancient Confucianism, so it could not be accepted as corresponding with the doctrines of Christianity. Therefore, the post-Han Confucianism needed Christianity to restore its original vitality. This need of Christianity was also made imperative because many of the ancient Confucian classics had been burned or lost during the Ch'in dynasty (221-207 B.C.). Besides accepting ancient Confucianism as a compatible religious system, the Jesuits also made compromises with the Chinese worship of ancestors and Confucius, considering these Chinese practices to carry only social and not religious implications.[3]

The result of the Jesuit religious work in China is truly impressive. Not only did they develop an effective intellectual dialogue with a significant segment of the Chinese literati, they also succeeded in gaining 200,000-300,000 Chinese converts at the beginning of the eighteenth century.[4] But their work finally suffered a devastating blow at the hands of the papacy in the eighteenth century. The papacy in a series of decrees in 1704, 1715, and 1742 rejected their theological accommodation with ancient Confucianism and forbade their allowance of the worship of ancestors and Confucius by the Chinese converts. The result of this papal prohibition was to reduce the Catholic influence in China, largely to the ordinary populace, and to cause Catholicism to fall to the wayside of Chinese political and cultural currents in the following two centuries. Catholicism was not restored as an important religious force until the twentieth century, when finally the papacy rescinded its earlier decrees in 1939.[5] As this story is rather well known, we shall not elaborate here.

Besides the Jesuits, another group of Europeans to treat Chinese culture and religion with respect and even admiration was the Sinophiles in the seventeenth and eighteenth centuries. Among them, G. W. Freiherr von Leibniz was one of the most outstanding representatives.

Dedicated to cultural and religious cosmopolitanism and admiring the rationalistic thinking of Confucianism, Leibniz formed a syncretic theory for the realisation of an accord between Christianity and Confucianism. He agreed with the Jesuits in acknowledging the religious nature of Confucianism and supported the Jesuit position with regard to the Chinese worship of ancestors and Confucius. He also engaged in the study of Confucianism. In a recent study of Leibniz, Professor David E. Mungello finds that Leibniz believed that several parallels existed in Western and Chinese cultures. Mungello describes some of these correspondences as follows. First, that *li* (principle) in Neo-Confucianism and the monads are 'each of a particular and a universal variety, the latter denoted by *t'ai'chi* and God, respectively'. Second, 'That *shang-ti, t'ien*, and *li* are near-equivalents of the Christian concept of God and that *t'ai-chi, li*, and *ch'i* (material force), taken together, correspond to the Christian Trinity'. Third, 'That the Chinese have a notion of an ethereal soul as distinct from a material soul and that this ethereal soul, sometimes called *ling-hun*, is close to the notion of a spiritual soul in Christianity'. Fourth, 'That the Chinese have a doctrine of reward and punishment after death in which *shang-ti* is the dispenser of justice and that this implies both the Christian concept of the immortality of the soul and divine justice'.[6]

From the above, we can see that Leibniz's position was in essential agreement with that of the Jesuits, except he had employed terms used in Neo-Confucian writings to argue his case.[7]

By the nineteenth century, the number of Western sympathisers and admirers of Chinese culture was drastically reduced. But there were still a few inheritors. For instance, James Legge, the great translator of the Chinese classics and a British missionary in China, supported the Jesuit position of equating Chinese *Shant-ti* with God, and thought that Confucianism was only 'defective' but not 'antagonistic' to Christianity.[8] Timothy Richard, another British missionary in China, also had a keen interest in Chinese culture. While stressing the superiority of Christianity as a spiritual system, he admitted that 'truth' could be found in Confucianism, Taoism and Buddhism.[9] He also praised the Confucian concept of moral government.[10] Besides being a cultural relativist, he was also a practitioner of social gospel. He made many efforts to spread Western scientific knowledge, and was even somewhat instrumental in the development of the Chinese reform movement of the late 1890s.[11]

But Legge and Richard were only a minority in the larger missionary community which largely consisted of Protestant fundamentalists. This larger group of missionaries (who refused to acknowledge any redemptive values in the Chinese culture and religions) ridiculed and denounced Legge and Richard.[12]

In the twentieth century the Western discussion or debate on China as a cultural and religious entity has been centring around two issues: the nature of Chinese culture and the related question of the legacy of Chinese scientific achievement, and the religious content of Chinese Confucianism and Maoism. We shall take up these issues by turn in the following discussion.

On the issue of the nature of Chinese culture or tradition, the Western evaluation began with some scattered and moderate appreciation in the early decades of the century, but has developed into a deep understanding and even great admiration in recent years.

In the 1920s Lord Bertrand Russell was a popular visitor in China and made extensive comments on China. To him, China in the 1920s was still a land of 'quiet rationalism characteristic of the eighteenth century', and 'an artist nation'. He believed that the Chinese had 'a civilization and a national temperament in many ways superior to those of white men'.[13] But Lord Russell also had some ambivalent feelings about China and the Chinese people. Inheriting some of the traditional European fears of an unpredictable East, he one time described what he called 'another side' of the Chinese people: 'They are capable of wild excitement, often of a collective kind. . . . It is this element in their character which makes them incalculable, and makes it impossible even to guess at their future. One can imagine a section of them becoming fanatically Bolshevik, or anti-Japanese, or Christian, or devoted to some leader who would eventually declare himself Emperor.'[14]

Speaking as early as in the 1920s, Russell's view could be considered as truly prophetic.

If this discussion of the relative merits and demerits in Chinese culture in the early decades was somewhat sporadic, a more serious evaluation has been made since the mid-century. Since then, many scholarly studies of Chinese culture have been published and many new issues raised. The intellectual depth of this new evaluation has reached a level that is unprecedented.

The most admirable example of the recent Western study of Chinese culture is a study of Neo-Confucianism made by Professor Thomas A. Metzger. His study is concerned with the spiritual predicament of the educated elites in the Ming-Ch'ing period (1368-1911) and with China's evolving political culture.

Professor Metzger's thesis of Chinese traditional culture and its problems is pitted mainly against that of Max Weber, Richard Solomon, Joseph Levenson and William Theodore de Bary.

Max Weber's interpretation of the nature of Chinese Confucianism is well known. In his view, Confucianism or Neo-Confucianism lacks an uplifting spiritual dynamism, and because of this lack, it could not provide enough tension or power to generate modernisation and capitalism in China. He believed this was the essential reason for China's backwardness in modern times.[15]

While accepting Weber's general theory of emphasis upon the relationship between modernisation and indigenous ethos, Metzger disagrees with Weber's interpretation of the nature of Confucianism or Neo-Confucianism. Metzger believes there is an ethos of interdependence in Neo-Confucianism which is not prohibitive to modernisation. Metzger describes this ethos under five 'headings': 'an ontology of elusive immanence; an epistemology emphasising the knowability of universal moral truth as an object of cognition and reasoning; a tendency toward "totalism" affecting ontological, epistemological, ethical, and social views; social norms involving a tension between notions of interdependence and authority; and a moral-psychological sense of living along a perilous divide between moral success and moral failure.'

Based on the above, Metzger considers that it is not an exaggeration to say that 'this ethos amounted to a comprehensive, continuing "religious faith"'.[16] Therefore, it is 'erroneous' for Weber to claim there is no tension or transformative orientation existing in Confucian or Neo-Confucian systems. What had hurt China's speed of modernisation was the existence of a sense of 'fatalism of the moral failure' in Neo-Confucianism and also the engagement of Chinese intellectuals in less transformative intellectual pursuits, such as the philosophical, phonological, and textual studies in the Ch'ing (1644-1911) times.[17] In other words, Neo-Confucianism itself did contain transformative orientations, though it also carried some elements or tendencies that were not entirely conducive to modernisation. Furthermore, because of the existence of such transformative orientations in the Chinese indigenous ethos, it explains why China has been more successful in modernisation than most of the Third World nations. In other words, whereas Weber was concerned with explaining China's failure in modernisation vis-à-vis the West, Metzger is interested in explaining its success vis-à-vis other Third World nations.[18]

Metzger also cannot accept Solomon's thesis of the existence of a 'dependency social orientation' in Confucian culture. Solomon describes Confucian culture as including these attitudes: an abhorrence of aggressive behaviour; a lack of 'self-esteem' and of confidence in one's own impulses and judgments; a placing of collective interests over individual ones; a sense of distrust permeating many social relations; and feelings of deference, impotence, anxiety, frustration, and anger toward authority, but not the notion of legitimated protest against those in authority.[19] In contrast to Solomon's emphasis on dependency and authoritarianism, Metzger speaks of 'the independent acts of moral self-assertion' in the Confucian ethos of interdependence.[20]

Toward Levenson's famous interpretation that modern Chinese culture was largely conditioned by the intrusion of the West and its ideas and values and that the Chinese insistence on the high value of their traditional culture was an effort to assuage their wounded cultural pride,[21] Metzger's position is instead on the opposite side. After having examined the shared cultural orientations in Neo-Confucianism, Metzger believes that such orientations have continued to dominate the content of modern Chinese intellectual thought down to present-day Maoism, and that the Chinese intellectuals' effort to uphold such orientations has not been an attempt to assuage their wounded pride but a demonstration of their genuine belief in them.[22]

Metzger's study of Neo-Confucianism is also methodologically different from that made by Professor William de Bary. To de Bary, the Neo-Confucian tradition, 'even more than a set moral code or philosophical system, was a life-style, an attitude of mind, a type of character formation, and spiritual ideal that eludes precise definition'. Furthermore, it brought to late imperial China 'an enlarged, more expansive view of what it means to be human'.[23] Whereas de Bary emphasises the universal insights and values in Neo-Confucianism, Metzger instead focuses on the 'metaphysical superstructure' of Neo-Confucianism. He believes that by studying the Neo-Confucian 'grammar' as 'a verbalised, culturally conditioned set of perceptions and claims',[24] we can find out the peculiar cultural orientations of the Chinese and balance the heretofore exclusive tendency in the study of Neo-Confucianism toward finding insights into the universal spiritual value of human existence. Only through such a study of the Neo-Confucian perceptions and claims, Metzger argues, can we understand 'the relation between their goals and their perception of the given world', their sense of predicament, and the meaning of their claims about how to escape from that predicament.[25]

Metzger's study of the Neo-Confucian ethos and predicament has indeed succeeded in demonstrating that there has been a striking continuity in the cultural concern of Chinese culture, from the medieval Neo-Confucian to the present thought of Mao Tse-tung, which he describes as also an effort to 'bridge the gap between the inner search for truth and outer transformative processes'.[26] In terms of comprehensiveness in scope and sophistication of analysis, Metzger's study can be considered as a landmark in the Western understanding of Chinese culture.

The related question of the legacy of Chinese scientific development has been a controversy in recent years. This controversy began with

Joseph Needham's publication of his multi-volumed *Science and Civilization in China*, whose first volume appeared in 1954. The thrust of Needham's work is twofold. First, by documenting the rich Chinese scientific heritage he tries to refute the cliché of stagnation of traditional China.[27] Second, by emphasising that Chinese science has 'an organic philosophy' which is in opposition to Western science as a mechanical materialism, he hopes to develop a concept of universal science in which both Chinese organism and Western mechanism are its integral parts.[28] In general, his critics are willing to acknowledge the rich Chinese scientific tradition, but not to accept Chinese traditional science as having contained the same crucial elements that made modern science possible.

In citing Chinese scientific contributions to the world, Needham has gone beyond the traditionally acknowledged list: paper making, printing, gunpowder, and magnetic compass. His new list of Chinese contributions now divides into four major areas: (*a*) explosives chemistry or protochemistry; (*b*) magnetic physics and the mariner's compass; (*c*) astronomical co-ordinates and instruments, mechanical clockworks, and the 'open' cosmology; (*d*) technological discoveries including the use of animal power with the inventions of the stirrup, the efficient equine harnesses, and the wheelbarrow; the use of water-power, with associated inventions such as the driving-belt, the chain-drive, the crank, and the morphology of the steam-engine; iron and steel technology, bridge-building, and deep drilling; nautical inventions such as the stern-post rudder, fore- and aft-sailing, the paddle-wheel boat, and watertight compartments.[29]

But why has Chinese science failed to develop into a scale as advanced as that in the modern West? Needham offers several main explanations. One is that Confucianism was so concerned with human affairs that it ignored the study of the natural world. Another is that though the Taoists had developed science and made many inventions, their scientific achievement could not sustain itself in a Confucian-dominated society and state. A Confucian feudal bureaucratism suppressed not only the scientific class but also mercantile democracy which had always served as a social basis for scientific development. Additionally, according to Needham, the founders of modern science, such as Kepler and Newton, all believed in a personal god and had a passion to seek out the divinely ordained law of nature; therefore, the lack of such a belief in Chinese thought had impeded their pursuit for the knowledge of the law of nature. A fourth explanation was that the Chinese conception of a 'law of nature' was understood by the Neo-Confucianists in a Whiteheadian, or organismic sense, and not in the Newtonian sense. And the failure to develop further the Chinese 'law of nature' was due to the fact that they had acquired 'a great distaste for abstractly codified law from their bad experiences with the Legalists'.[30]

Many scientists and historians of science have criticised Needham's findings and explanations. Their criticisms can be divided into two categories. One is concerned with Needham's definition of science or modern scientific development, and the other with Needham's explanations for China's failure to develop science in modern times.

For Nathan Sivin, the concepts and attitude embedded in the Chinese traditional scientific disciplines were drastically different from that of the West in 'aim, approach, and organisation', and missed 'the notion of rigorous demonstration, of proof'.[31] Shigeru Nakayama criticises Needham's underestimation of the role played by mathematics in the establishment of a mathematico-mechanistic view of Nature, which was synonymous with the seventeenth-century Scientific Revolution. Nakayama also finds that traditional China did not create ' a unified view of, and approach to, Nature', therefore, 'Chinese science and technology remained an unorganised mass of fragmentary empirical knowledge lacking a nucleus up to the beginning of Westernisation'.[32]

Among the critics that have refuted Needham's explanations for China's failure to develop science in modern times, Lewis S. Feuer's criticism is probably the most extensive. Feuer does not agree with Needham's interpretation that Confucian human concern had been the cause for the retardation of Chinese scientific development. Feuer points out that the human or social concern of Voltaire, Hume, and Benjamin Franklin did not detract them from their interest in the natural sciences. What was harmful for scientific development was the psychological repression of human desires in Confucianism. Democracy was also not necessarily a prerequisite for scientific development. There is evidence to show that in those European towns where science flourished, there were more oligarchies or aristrocracies than democracies.

The lack of the belief in a personal god in Chinese thought also was not a factor that prevented China from developing modern science. Feuer argues that the image of God in Kepler and Newton was 'a seventeenth-century impersonal rationality', which was certainly not a personal deity. Therefore, whether Chinese elites had a personal god or not was really not an important issue. Feuer further argues against the attribution of the Chinese distaste for a systematic code of law as a reason for the Chinese failure to develop a conception of a law of nature. He points out that science had made great advances in England where the English common law had just as great an aversion to systems and codes as the Chinese.[33]

In conclusion, Feuer offers his own theory to explain the Chinese failure to develop modern science—a theory of hedonistic and libertarian individualism. In his view, such a hedonistic and libertarian individualism was the primal mover for the Western scientific development; but in China, its ethic system had repressed the emotional energies and thwarted the natural direction of sexuality, therefore, scientific movement could not be sustained.[34]

Next, we shall turn to the issue of Western evaluation of the religious content of Chinese Confucianism, Neo-Confucianism, and Maoism in the twentieth century. Both in medieval times and during the present there is no disagreement among Western observers that both Buddhism and Taoism are genuine religions. What has been at issue is whether Confucianism or Neo-Confucianism can be considered as a religion. In the early decades of the twentieth century, many European scholars continued the eighteenth-century interpretation that there was no transcendent element but only rationalism or moral maxims in Neo-Confucianism.[35] Since their discussion of this issue was rather limited and superficial, we shall not dwell upon it. But in recent years, a new interpretation has been advanced which affirms such a religiosity in the Confucian system. Furthermore, there is a new twist in this contemporary affirmation. Whereas those Western sympathisers of Chinese culture such as Ricci only accepted such a religiosity in ancient Confucianism, the new admirers would go beyond ancient Confucianism and include Neo-Confucianism as also containing genuine religious essence. Two representatives of this new interpretation are Ninian Smart and Huston Smith.

For Smart, Confucius was certainly not an agnostic, but a religious and moral reformer. Confucius truly believed in a supreme providential being, though not in divine determinism or naturalistic fatalism. As for Chu Hsi and Wang Yang-ming, the two greatest Neo-Confucians in medieval China, they had continued the Confucian ethical concern, but they also adopted some Buddhist and Taoist concepts and practices to enrich ancient Confucianism. Smart points out that Chu Hsi's idea of the Great (Supreme) Ultimate (*T'ai-chi*) was close to Taoist ideas and his concept of *li* 'reflected Buddhist notions of the Buddha-nature residing within living beings'. As for the philosophy of Wang Yang-ming, its method of relying upon meditative techniques to arrive at *li* 'bore something of the imprint of Meditation Buddhism'. All in all, Smart concludes that because of the close relation between Confucianism and Chinese ancient cults and its later incorporation of many Buddhist and Taoist concepts and practices, Confucianism 'forms part of the fabric of the religion of China'.[36]

Professor Smith's contribution to the study of the religious aspects of Chinese culture is his succinct analysis of the element of transcendence in traditional Chinese thought. He also affirms the religiosity in the man Confucius and in the body of philosophy that is called Confucianism. The following statement captures the essence of Smith's thesis:

Confucius carefully kept the numinous alive, in his admonition to 'respect the spiritual beings', in his close attention to sacrificial ceremonies, in his watchfulness toward Heaven and its decrees. The formalised Confucianism about which we sometimes read, the Confucianism that is all exterior with no sensitivity to inwardness and the hidden mystery into which all of life's roots ultimately invisibly descend—this is fossilised Confucianism where it is Confucianism at all. The *li* which stood at the heart of Confucianism-alive was a tap-root fixed in the mystery of the Tao which, where not cut by selfishness, kept both individuals and society in living touch with Heaven's majestic will.[37]

Smith finds five major points in the metaphysics of the Chinese literati. One, men and heaven are real in both the phenomenal and the noumenal realm. Two, the essential relation between men and heaven is unity or non-duality. Thus, the many Chinese terms, such as *li*, *ming* (ordinance), *tao*, *teh* (power), and *yang-yin*, 'apply to Heaven and man equally'; and other terms, such as *ti* (God), *ch'i*, *t'ai-chi*, and *wu-chi* (non-polarity), 'refer primarily to Heaven but are manifest and function in man also'. Three, in Chinese thought the theme of mutual reciprocity 'is in most instances between unequals, the relations that link man and nature are not symmetrical'. Four, though the Chinese perspective is humanistic, it places man against a 'noumenal backdrop'. And five, whereas in ancient Chinese thought the numinous was a personified one, it later became blurred and the Chinese literati tried to reach it through allusion and senses.[38] Professor Smith believes that the psychological benefits flowing from the Confucian concept of transcendence have reinforced the social conduct of the Chinese.[39]

If Confucianism does indeed contain a religious dimension, how about Maoism or the thought of Mao Tse-tung? On this question, divergent views have been expressed and they have created another controversy. We shall start first with those views that have affirmed the religiosity of Maoism or Maoist thought.

In a paper delivered at an ecumenical conference on China and the West held in 1977,[40] Raymond L. Whitehead, Director of Canada China Programme of the Canadian Council of Churches, has presented probably some of the most straightforward and assertive statements concerning the religious elements in Maoism or Maoist culture. Based on his very favourable assessment of the record of the Chinese Communist revolution, which he considers as having been 'a movement toward genuine liberation, greater justice, and a revitalised common morality', he suggests seven propositions for looking at the nature of Maoism or Maoist China. For our purpose, we shall only mention three of them. One is that since 'to a significant extent justice is done and the broken are healed' in the Maoist revolution, 'salvation' or 'God's saving power' is to be found in China. Another is that even though the Chinese people today are almost universally not Christians, the spiritual reality of faith, hope, love, struggle, and sacrifice is not absent among them. Lastly, though 'salvation is not complete in Maoism', neither is it complete in the Christian Church. Therefore, a useful dialogue can be developed between Maoism and the Church. In such a dialogue, we should certainly pay attention to what Maoists do and say, but we should also look seriously at the Chinese charge of cultural imperialism that was committed by Western missions, re-evaluate Christian identification with bourgeois individuation and learn the lessons from Chinese medical and educational reforms made in recent years.[41]

Probably no one, however, can surpass the enthusiasm of Joseph Needham in asserting the existence of an intense religiosity in Maoism or Maoist culture.

In his view, Maoist China is not only religious, but also Christian-like, for the Chinese society is 'nearer to, further on the way to, the true society of mankind, the Kingdom of God if you like, than our own', and China as a whole is 'the only truly Christian country in the world at the present day, in spite of its absolute rejection of all religion'. What are the evidences? To answer this question, Needham quotes Lancelot Andrewes's catalogue of divine actions and attributes as things that have happened on mainland China: 'Opening the eyes of the blind, clothing the naked, upholding such as fall, gathering together the outcasts, giving food to the hungry, bringing down the haughty, delivering the captives, releasing the prisoners, lifting up those that are down, healing the sick, sustaining the living and quickening the dead, raising the lowly and helping in time of trouble.'

To Needham, to find Christ is to find 'where the good are, and where good things are done'; since he believes all those good things listed by Andrewes have already happened in China, China therefore is certainly the only Christian country *par excellence*.[42]

A Jesuit father from Holy Cross College in Massachusetts, U.S.A., also joined Whitehead and Needham in offering high praises for Maoist China. Rev. William van Etten Casey filed a touching report in 1975 on life in China: 'As I watched the people rising and retiring early, enjoying their few simple pleasures, relying on one another for help and encouragement, convincing each other of goals and means, living an ascetical life in the Spartan society cut off from the rest of the world, I could not help but think of the new China as a huge Jesuit Novitiate of the 1930s where the people, like Jesuit novices, worked diligently, intently, and sometimes awkwardly, at developing their virtues'.[43] So China of today is a religious community or kingdom!

The sanguine, religious perspective as described above can certainly not pass without being challenged by the conservative or 'orthodox' Christian observers of China, and challenges have indeed been forthcoming from various quarters.

Professor Charles C. West of Princeton Theological Seminary has offered detailed criticism of such a perspective based on the traditional (or 'orthodox') understanding of the Christian faith. To him, to identify Maoism or Maoist revolution as the true expression of God's salvation and to pay no attention to the Communist suppression of the Christian Church and gospel in China is 'idolatry' and 'a worship of human objects in the name of God'.[44] West believes that the Bible has shown a pattern of interaction between God's salvation and human struggle. As shown in the Bible, Christian salvation depended on God's power and was realised according to God's plan, not through human effort. Human struggle for social liberation comes after God's calling man into a covenant with himself and is 'controlled both in its method and goals' by God. Otherwise, no liberation can be achieved, but the substitution of a new tyranny for the old. Furthermore, since in the Bible God called his people to repentance and self-transformation, 'the test of the trustworthiness of any earthly power, conservative or revolutionary' is to see whether 'this openness to repentance and reform is effectively present'. Lastly, West points out that the dominant theme of history is that through God's grace man is reconciled with God and peace as the goal of the kingdom of God is realised. Therefore, human struggle for liberation conceived in human ideologies cannot be equated with God's salvation. Revolution by coercive power is not a means of grace.[45]

Based on these understandings, West suggests that as Christians we should look at today's China in the following ways. First, though the radicalism of China can be considered as 'the world's most drastic response to 2,000 years of the Christian mission', its humanisation of God's power into the power of the Party will not be an 'adequate vehicle', for such a power 'is morally and spiritually ambiguous'. Second, we should accept that the events of twentieth-century China are a judgment of God on the Western missionary church which has failed to generate 'an effective Christian critique of power and Christian social movement'. Third, even if we admit the tremendous material progress that has been made in Maoist China, we should continue to hope there will be more 'openness' in China and the restoration of 'freedom of religion, freedom to relate to the past, and freedom to communicate with people of other ideologies and societies'. Fourth, we should defer to the experience and judgment of Chinese Christians to seek and verify the meaning of Maoism for history.[46]

Professor Creighton Lacy of Duke University also disagrees with the euphoric interpretation of Maoism or Maoist China, especially that advanced by Whitehead. Lacy's criticisms have, in the main, focused on Whitehead's concepts of salvation and Maoism. Lacy disputes Whitehead's identifying Maoist liberation with salvation, for the latter depends on a knowledge of and loyalty to Jesus of Nazareth and is much more encompassing and complete. Concerning Maoism, Lacy not only raises the issue of human cost resulting from the struggle principle in Maoism, but also its one-sided interpretation of, and exclusive claim to, truth.[47]

But the most hostile critic of the religious interpretation of Maoism of Maoist China is probably Professor Donald W. Treadgold, a prominent historian from the University of Washington. Treadgold also has his seven propositions, which he terms as 'mistakes' that have been committed by some Christians in assessing the relationship between China and Christianity over the past several centuries. One of their major mistakes is their view that 'the P.R.C. (People's Republic of China) represents something like the march of God in history'.

Treadgold's perspective is truly that of a historian in comparing today's religious Sinophiles with those that had heaped praises on Soviet Russia after the Bolshevik Revolution. For Treadgold, the identification of Maoist China with the salvation in the Christian sense is simply making what Eric Voegelin has called 'the error of confusing saved and profane history, of divining human events, including the most calamitous and brutal actions of man'. Treadgold cites many calamitous and brutal actions in Maoist China. In addition to the repression of free thought and religion, the Chinese Communist regime has caused the death of at least 30 million, and locked up 40 million in concentration camps. (Lest some would disagree with these estimates, he reminds them that similar estimates made on Stalinist persecutions were eventually vindicated.) He also cautions those in the West not to believe in the image of the 'New Man' having been created in Maoist China; he quotes one Chinese Christian's testimony as proof: 'In recent years, some Western scholars have tended to describe people in Communist China as a kind of "New Man", with newly acquired qualities of devoted service and self-sacrifice, faithfully following Chairman Mao's moral exhortations in pursuit of lofty social goals. This, however, is mainly the view of deluded observers from outside.' Treadgold at the end of his criticism appeals to Christians to be inspired by their 'ideal of liberation from fear of oppression' and to stand by the side of the suffering Chinese people.[48]

II

The above survey of the Western perception of Chinese culture indicates that, with the exception of the nineteenth century, this perception has been a favourable one. Confucianism as a spiritual system means different things to different Western reviewers. It is considered either as a rationalistic philosophy, a social ethic, or even an authentic religion. Whatever it is, Confucianism is recognised as a valuable part of the human cultural heritage.

But we should understand that this favourable Western evaluation of Chinese culture does not extend itself into other aspects of the Chinese civilisation. For instance, the Chinese political system has not always been perceived in a very positive light. The concept of Oriental despotism has been accepted by many Westerners as a common denominator of Chinese political development throughout its history.[49] As a political entity, China has been viewed by the West as a menace to be feared (the concepts of Yellow Peril and the Red Terror); or as a corruption to be despised (the images of the obnoxious Mandarins in the nineteenth century and the internecine warlords in the first half of the twentieth century). This is another side of the Western perception of China that should be kept in mind as a contrast with their favourable evaluation of Chinese culture.

But why has the West developed this favourable evaluation of Chinese culture? The answer to this question, of course, is not an easy one. Besides the intrinsic value of Chinese culture, the other cause may be found in the psychology of the Western man himself. Henri Baudet in his illuminating treatise on the European images of non-European man has argued that the relation of European to non-European man has been governed more intensively and more compellingly by 'an inner urge', stemming from 'nostalgia for the deep, the ideal, the ultimate harmony still cherished as the real purpose of the Creation'. To seek this harmony, the Western man has sought it either in his historical past or in a world outside the West. Therefore, in the eighteenth century, 'with a protesting attitude toward the whole of history' Western man 'felt so strongly attracted to the other world'. And in the nineteenth century, he was more satisfied with his achievements and 'was historically oriented', so he did not try 'to seek Paradise beyond the horizon'.[50]

If we accept this analysis, and the present author tends to do so, what has been discussed in this historical survey will become clear to us. The favourable evaluation of Chinese culture made by the Enlightenment Sinophiles was a result of their disappointment with the religious, social, and political developments on their own continent. To them, the existence of a superstitious and suffocating religion or theology, the social privileges enjoyed by the clergy and the aristocratic classes, and the constant bickerings and warfares among the European states were all in sharp contrast with what China was offering to the world: a philosophy that was rationalistic and ethical; a social recognition that was based on achievement through a fair examination system; and above all, a unified political system that had maintained law and order in the Chinese empire.[51] Even Chinese arts and living styles were also considered to be superior to those of the West, and thus we saw the emergence in the West of the Rococo style and fashion that was called *Chinoiserie*.[52]

During the nineteenth and the early decades of the twentieth century the West was dominating the world in almost every sphere of human achievement and was extremely confident of itself in both material and spiritual matters. In recent years, however, we have witnessed a renewal of the early euphoria about China and Chinese culture. Not only the Maoist revolution is viewed by some as a great human liberation and even salvation, Maoism and Chinese culture have also been very well received. Whatever the merits or demerits of Maoist China and Chinese culture, the background of this new euphoria is certainly the development of doubt and disappointment with what has been happening in contemporary Western society. Simon Leys (Pierre Ryckmans), a Sinologist and an admirer of the Chinese humanistic tradition whose Sinophilism is of a different anchoring and perspective from that of Joseph Needham, has made the following comments:

> 'Western ideologues now use Maoist China just as the eighteenth-century philosophers used Confucian China: as a myth, an abstract ideal projection, a utopia which allows them to denounce everything that is bad in the West without taking the trouble to think for themselves. We stifle in the miasma of industrial civilisation, our cities rot, our roads are blocked by the insane proliferation of cars, *et cetera*. So they hurry to celebrate the People's Republic, where pollution, delinquency, and traffic problems are non-existent. One might as well praise an amputee because his feet aren't dirty.'[53]

And Leys has further quoted Lu Hsün, that greatest modern Chinese 'cultural psychiatrist', to show the proper way for a Westerner to react to present-day China: 'Thus, if a foreigner could be found today who, though admitted to the Chinese banquet, would not hesitate to rant in our name against the present state of China, he I would call a truly honest man, a truly admirable man!'[54]

We do not have to accept Ley's advice or what he has called his 'sterile sarcasm'[55] as a basis to view Maoist China or Maoist culture. In this matter, Leys may have just as much bias as anybody else. Therefore, one way to outgrow or bypass all the stereotypes in the Western evaluation of China and its culture, past and present, is to listen to what the Chinese people today on the mainland have said about them. If nothing else, what they have said can at least serve as references for us. In this instance, some recent wallposters appearing on the Tienanmen (heavenly peace) Square in Peking may shed some light for us. A 'Manifesto' issued by a group called the *Ch'i-meng She* (the enlightenment society) and pasted up to November 24, 1978 has declared its twelve articles of faith as guidances for the realisation of 'democracy and human rights' in China, and we shall only translate two of them as follows:

> The feudal society and the dictatorial country of the Ch'in Shih Huang-ti [the First Emperor of the Ch'in Dynasty, 221-207 B.C.] were gone forever. The blind worship of the East has to be rejected, and as [we] people are no more 'dummies', so we must launch a full attack against the remnants of the dictatorial Fascism.

And,

> There are presently two Great Walls. One was built to prevent foreign enemies from invasion [of China]. The other is the spiritual Great Wall that has been erected by the sons and grandsons of the Ch'in Shih Huang-ti to protect their dictatorial system. . . . As for the latter, it has to be demolished.[56]

As the true heirs of the Chinese tradition and culture, the voice of these twentieth-century sons of the Han, in this author's view, has to be taken seriously by any Western observer of China, irrespective of his own inclinations towards China and Chinese culture.

Lastly, we will also say a few words about the Western discussion of the legacy of Chinese scientific development. In this author's view, Western interpretations of China's failure to develop science, modernisation, or capitalism are all useful explanations for this failure. But none of the interpretations gives a full answer to this failure. The author believes that the perennial preoccupation of the Chinese literati with the pursuit of fortunes in the Chinese officialdom through passing the civil service examination may have exhausted the best energy of this class. Furthermore, their daily engagements in what Metzger has called the less transformative pursuits, such as *shih* (poetry), *shu* (scholarly study of philosophical, phonological and textual subjects), *ch'in* (music), *hua* (painting), have also used up their remaining energies. These double pursuits of the Chinese literati had probably more than anything else retarded the Chinese development of science, modernisation, and capitalism. The author thinks that these double pursuits should be given much more attention than they received in either Weber's theory of the Protestant ethic or Metzger's illustration of the Confucian 'predicament' as a way to explain China's failure to catch up with the West in the development of science, modernisation and capitalism.

Notes

1. The most useful studies of the Jesuit work in China in the English language are: A. H. Rowbotham *Missionary and Mandarin* (Berkeley and Los Angeles 1942); G. H. Dunne *Generation of Giants* (Notre Dame, Indiana 1962); and D. W. Treadgold *The West in Russia and China*, Vol. 2, China, 1582-1949 (New York 1973), 1-34. Among the Chinese materials, see *Fang Hao liu-shih tzu-ting kao* (The collected works of Maurus Fang Hao, revised and edited by the author on his sixtieth birthday) (Tapei 1969).

2. Ch'en Shou-i 'Ming-mo Ch'ing-ch'u Yeh-ssu hui shih ti ju-chiao kuan chi ch'i fan-ying (The Confucian views of the Jesuits in the late Ming and early Ch'ing times and their repercussions)' in *Kuo-li Pei-ching ta-hsüeh kuo-hsüeh chi-k'an* (The Chinese studies quarterly of National Peking University) 5 (2):1-10.

3. Ibid. pp. 14-31.

4. W. Franke *China and the West* (New York 1967) p. 48.

5. Fang Hao op. cit. pp. 205-206; D. W. Treadgold op. cit. pp. 30-4.

6. D. E. Mungello *Leibniz and Confucianism: The Search for Accord* (Honolulu 1977) pp. 116-17.

7. Ibid. pp. 72-5.

8. D. W. Treadgold op. cit. p. 43.

9. Ibid. p. 61.

10. P. R. Bohr *Famine in China and the Missionary* (Cambridge, Mass. 1972) p. 158.

11. D. W. Treadgold op. cit. pp. 56-65.

12. Ibid. pp. 43, 60-2.

13. Ibid. pp. 230, 138.

14. N. Cameron *Barbarians and Mandarins* (Chicago 1979) p. 408.

15. M. Weber *The Religion of China* (New York 1964); see especially C. K. Yang's 'Introduction' to this reprint edition.

16. T. A. Metzger *Escape from Predicament* (New York 1977) p. 197.

17. Ibid. pp. 204, 127-34, 161-65.

18. Ibid. pp. 234-35.

19. Ibid. p. 239.

20. Ibid. p. 15.

21. Ibid. pp. 6, 7, 11, 30, 221-22.

22. Ibid.

23. Ibid. pp. 54-5.

24. Ibid. p. 54.

25. Ibid. pp. 59-60.

26. Ibid. p. 231.

27. R. Dawson, ed. *The Legacy of China* (London 1964) pp. 234-41.

28. S. Nakayama and N. Sivin, ed. *Chinese Science* (Cambridge, Mass. 1973) pp. 39-40.

29. R. Dawson op. cit. p. 257.

30. L. S. Feuer *The Scientific Intellectual* (New York 1963) pp. 240-42.

31. Nakayama and Sivin op. cit. pp. xxvii, 62.

32. Ibid. pp. 33-4.

33. L. S. Feuer op. cit. pp. 243-52.

34. Ibid. pp. 252-53.

35. Chang Ch'in-shih, ed. *Kuo-nei chin-shih-nien-lai chih tsung-chiao ssu-ch'ao* (The tide of religious thought in China during the last decade) (Peking 1927) pp. 147-54.

36. N. Smart *The Religious Experience of Mankind* (New York 1969) pp. 151-52, 186-90.

37. H. Smith 'Transcendence in Traditional China' *Religious Studies* 2 (1 & 2) (1967) pp. 187-88.

38. Ibid. pp. 188-91.

39. Ibid. p. 192.

40. R. L. Whitehead 'Christ, Salvation, and Maoism', a paper delivered at the Notre Dame Conference on China and the West: *The Religious Dimension* June 29-July 2, 1977.

41. Ibid. pp. 1-14.

42. J. Needham 'Christian Hope and Social Evolution' *China Notes* 12 (2) (Spring 1974) pp. 13-20.

43. W. van Etten Casey, S.J. 'Mao's China' *Holy Cross Quarterly* 7 (1-4) (1975) p. 10.

44. C. C. West 'Some Theological Reflections on China' *China Notes* 14 (4) (Fall 1976) p. 39.

45. West 'Theological Reflections on China—II' (a paper circulated at the Notre Dame Conference on China and the West) pp. 2-4.

46. Ibid. pp. 4-7.

47. C. Lacy 'A Response to "Christ, Salvation and Maoism"' *China Notes* 15 (4) (Fall 1977) pp. 7-10.

48. D. W. Treadgold 'The Problem of Christianity in Non-Western Cultures: The Case of China' a keynote speech delivered at the Notre Dame Conference, pp. 12-16.

49. The most celebrated example is K. A. Wittfogel *Oriental Despotism* (New Haven, Conn. 1957).

50. H. Baudet *Paradise on Earth* (New Haven, Conn. 1965) pp. 74-5.

51. G. F. Hudson *Europe and China* (London 1931) pp. 313-29; W. Franke op. cit. pp. 59-65.

52. Hudson op. cit. 270-90; H. Honour *Chinoiserie* (New York 1961).

53. S. Leys *Chinese Shadows* (New York 1977) p. 201.

54. Ibid.; it is cited on the page before 'Foreword'.

55. Ibid. p. 211.

56. *The United Daily* (Taipei, Taiwan), November 26, 1978. The story of this Enlightenment Society was reported by Japanese news media in Tokyo.

Julia Ching

The Chinese Religious Sense

THE Chinese have been variously characterised by missionaries and scholars, native and Western, past and present, as either religious and theistic, or irreligious, atheistic and this-worldly. In the seventeenth and eighteenth centuries, this division of opinion conditioned the strife that began among missionary circles and spread into European philosophical circles: the so-called Ritual Controversy, regarding the permissibility of 'Chinese Rites' to Christians, and the so-called Terms Controversy, regarding the manner of rendering into Chinese the word 'God'. Jesuits and Dominicans took one or the other side. The philosophers were likewise divided. Leibniz regarded the Chinese as religious and theistic, but derived his judgment partly from reading the treatise of the Jesuit missionary Longobardi, who tended to favour the other side. Christian Wolff, Leibniz' good friend, praised the Chinese for their 'natural morality', one grounded in strictly philosophical concepts, with no reference to religion and no belief in God.[1] A Chinese scholar of more recent times[2] says of his own people that they are 'unreligious', and his opinion is confirmed by various Western scholars. Joseph Needham, the eminent historian of science and himself a religious person, emphasised that the Chinese did not possess a belief in God similar to that of the West—a Creator-God and Lawgiver—thus echoing the judgment of the philosopher Filmer Northrop.[3] On the other hand, scholarly articles have been written on the very notion of the Chinese belief in God, and research continues on this subject. Archaeology continues to unearth evidence in support of an early religious theism. And while it lies beyond the scope of this paper to analyse theologically the meaning of God in Western Christianity, before discussing the Chinese case, it is my presupposition that the word 'God' should refer, in both East and West, to a supreme deity who is in control of human and terrestrial affairs.

19

Instead of dismissing the problem of such co-existing contradictions by appealing to varying understandings and definitions of 'religion', I propose to discuss the question of the distinctive 'religious sense' of the Chinese, the uniqueness of which has provoked such differing appraisals. I shall proceed by examining the arguments of Chinese 'this-worldliness' *versus* others' 'other-worldliness', of Chinese 'atheism' *versus* 'theism', and of a supposed formalistic, external, morality *versus* an internalised sense of guilt grounded in religion. I shall conclude with a response to these problems, discussing the Chinese religious sense in terms of transcendence/immanence, while touching also upon a historical and political problem.

1. THIS-WORLDLY *VERSUS* OTHER-WORLDLY

This is the most frequent category of discussion for those who compare the Chinese and their mentality to others—and others include not just Western Christians, but also and especially Indians, the neighbours of the Chinese across the Himalayas. Max Weber[4] remarks on the Chinese tendency toward and preference for harmony with nature and society. The philosopher Liang Su-ming[5] judges the Chinese as this-worldly, in comparison to the Indians, the people who have produced the Vedic Scriptures, the Gita, as well as Buddhism. The Japanese Buddhologist Hajime Nakamura[6] says likewise. These appraisals are, moreover, supported by the presence of historical documents: indeed, the Chinese fondness for this world and this life is evident in the fact that the Chinese possess detailed historical records going back several millennia, whereas the Indians never bothered very much to put down great events of the past, so that scholars continue to debate over historical chronology for well-known events in Indian history, known, indeed, on account of *other* material than written records, whether tablets or coinage.

If the assumption here is that 'this-worldliness' refers to a predominant concern for this world and this life, and the affirmation of certain values usually regarded as secular, then the general consensus in this regard appears to be correct. However, concern for, and affirmation of, this life and this world need not *exclude* beliefs regarding what may come after this life and this world. The veneration of ancestors is a good indication of this sense of the beyond, a veneration which was regarded as idolatrous by certain missionaries—and idolatry can hardly be termed a purely *secular* indulgence. There is, besides, the evidence of classical and historical documents, of art and artifacts, that cannot be easily dismissed as unreligious or 'this-worldly'. Even the characteristically Chinese concern in painting as well as architecture for 'harmony' with nature, which contrasts so vividly with Western art and architecture—to mention only the medieval cathedrals—does not necessarily bespeak mere 'secularity'. Is not the Temple of Heaven in Peking an obvious place of worship, even though the *style* of worship, incorporated into the architecture itself, is distinctive?

Such worship indeed, calls to mind the important argument regarding alleged Chinese 'a-theism'. Prayer texts of the Emperor's worship of Heaven[7] clearly manifest a belief in a supra-mundane deity, even a 'personal' deity. How, then, can these arguments be at all justified?

2.   GOD *VERSUS* NO GOD

As the word *religio* refers to the relationship between man and God, the ultimate arguments on religiosity will have to be that of belief in God. Mention has already been made of certain persons, scholars and missionaries, who judged the Chinese to be a-theists. When one remembers that this general statement supposedly covers thousands of years of cultural history as well as billions of persons, one cannot but be staggered by the boldness of the assertion.

Frequently the argument is made on *a priori* grounds. The Chinese *cannot* be theists, because their national character or language does not allow it. Such is the line of argumentation maintained by Needham and Northrop. It at once suggests that *only* certain national types or languages allow belief in God, presumably those deriving from the Indo-European, or the Semitic. Even more at stake is perhaps a rather narrow notion of God and belief, so-called classical theism, as evinced in the Jewish and Christian Scriptures, for example.

The answer to this argument becomes clear on analysis of the question itself: *must* belief in God necessarily be belief in the Jewish-Christian God, and *is* this necessarily a 'personal' deity? Of course, even in the latter case, one might refer to the cult of Heaven in China. And in any case, the very disagreement between missionaries and scholars of the past and present is enough to cast suspicion on 'monolithic' answers. Why and how can one characterise a people and a civilization with a long historic past, and stretching across half a continent, as 'having always been', and 'by necessity' atheist? Is it not possible that there are, and have been, *both* believers and non-believers of God in China? Is it also not possible, that a more personal notion of God was predominant at certain periods and within certain circles, while a more 'transpersonal' notion became prevalent at other periods and within certain other circles?

The Terms controversy which plagued Catholic missionary efforts during the seventeenth and eighteenth centuries, and then flared up again among Protestant missionaries of the late nineteenth and early twentieth centuries is itself instructive. The difficulty of translating 'God' into Chinese lies in the fact that the language offers many words which may stand for 'God', but not one of these is 'perfectly suitable'. Is this not on account of a *distinctive* notion of God—a God of many names, one might say, a God who cannot be simply captured by any *one term*?

One problem deserving mention and study is both historical and political: the 'royal' monopoly of God in China. According to Confucian teachings, the ruler receives his political mandate from Heaven, and may lose it if he misgoverns or misbehaves. The ruler used to be called Son of Heaven. He alone could offer sacrifice to Heaven, although on behalf of his people and realm. Commoners who attempted to do so—or even remotely claimed some special relationship to Heaven—were therefore guilty of treason. This historical fact explains why prayer was not as much a part of the life of the ordinary people as it was that of the sages and kings—at least, where records[8] are concerned. It also explains why 'minor gods' flourished in popular cults: the supreme Heaven itself appeared so distant to the humble and lowly. And it explains the political suspicion of popular cults, and the supervision of religious activities. This is true not only of the distant past, but also of the present. The Chinese term for 'revolution' remains *ko-ming*—removal of the Mandate, a Mandate from Heaven. Colloquial language offers the term *pien-t'ien*: to change Heaven, to change Heaven's Mandate. True, Heaven has many meanings: personal deity, moral force, nature, the sky—perhaps as hierophany of the divine. The simultaneous presence of many meanings does not, however, deny the importance of a primary meaning: the word itself was originally represented by the symbol for a man with a big head: the supreme and anthropomorphic deity.

3.   SHAME *VERSUS* GUILT MORALITY

It has also been asserted that the Chinese lack an 'internalised' sense of morality, that they do things for the sake of face, and face alone, that they only feel shame, not guilt. I have in mind here not only the assertions of anthropologists like Ruth Benedict,[9] but also the arguments regarding the lack of a sense of sin, which missionaries mentioned in connection with another 'linguistic gap': that there is no proper Chinese equivalent for 'sin', since the term *tsui*, refers to formal crime. In spite of various scholarly publications, such as W. Eberhard's study on *Guilt and Sin in*

Traditional China, as well as H. Maspero's examination of Taoist penitential rituals,[10] this assertion has left behind a real residue. I should like to mention additional evidence: that of the Confucian classics, for example, including the prayers of the sage kings of the past who asked for mercy for their people, assuming on themselves the 'sins' of their subjects. There is also the little known passage, present in *both* the Doctrine of the Mean and the Great Learning, regarding moral vigilance in solitude: the gentleman watches over himself even when he is alone.

It has even been asserted that the Chinese are not prone to experience moral conflicts, since there is little record of these in literature. This argument can perhaps be more easily answered. Must inner experiences be recorded to be acknowledged? During the decade of the Great Proletarian Cultural Revolution, which began around 1964, little mention was made of romantic motifs in literature either. Does it mean the Chinese did not 'love' during those years, or just that they made it a private affair? Could the relative lack of conflict in literature also be explained by a certain reticence? Silence is not a UNIVOCAL answer.

4. A RESPONSE

In examining certain issues, I have acknowledged the 'this-worldly' orientation of the Chinese while qualifying it in my own way. I have answered the theist/a-theist dichotomy by asserting the possibility of an entire spectrum of beliefs regarding God or divinity. And I have attempted to refute the shame *versus* guilt argument by reference to classical proofs. Now I wish to discuss the distinctiveness of the Chinese religious sense itself: this very elusive quality which characterises the Chinese attitude toward God, the world, and moral responsibility. I propose to do so in terms of transcendence and immanence, or rather, in the Chinese context, in terms of a transcendence which is present in spite of 'this-worldly' orientations.

Mahayana Buddhists, including those of the Ch'an (Zen) persuasion, like to speak of 'Nirvana' being present in 'Samsara'—the latter referring to the cycle of transmigration affecting all sentient beings. It marks a distinctive difference between Mahayana adherents and those of the Theravada school, for whom Nirvana, the beyond, the absolute, *transcends* Samsara, the realm of relativity. The Mahayana formulation represents indeed a total revolution in Buddhist thinking: the affirmation of this-worldly values which does not bring with it the negation of the values of the beyond. While articulated already in the second century A.D. by Nagarjurna, of the Middle Doctrine or Madhyamika school, it caught the imagination of Chinese and Japanese Buddhists, and even of Cunfucians and Neo-Confucians, Taoists and Neo-Taoists. According to this statement, the sacred is believed to be present in the profane, the absolute in the relative, and mystical enlightenment itself in humdrum daily duties. It enabled a somewhat 'secularist' liberation for the Buddhists, making the attainment of Buddhahood a universal possibility, even for the laity, while it strengthened further the ethical commitments of Confucianism, and modified the excessive zeal of those Taoists preoccupied with the quest for immortality.

To those who claim and argue that the Chinese tradition has not known of a dimension of religious 'transcendence', this formula offers an answer in paradoxical language. It illustrates the need for a 'dialectical' understanding of China—one that goes beyond affirmations and negations, without denying the usefulness of some affirmations and some negations. Chinese 'this-worldliness', Chinese harmony between man and nature, man and the world, Chinese preference for the human and the ethical, bespeak a kind of 'divine immanence', the presence of the absolute in the relative, in human relationships, in the realm of the natural. But the transcendent is not excluded. It is, indeed, highlighted since it gives meaning to the ordinary and the natural, the secular and the moral. This distinctive Chinese religious sense aims indeed at a harmonious balance of two worlds, the visible as well as the invisible, the temporal as well as the supra-temporal. But it directs the human person to seek his salvation, or even his perfection, in the here and now, particularly in the morality of human relationships as with Confucianism, but also in the beauty of nature as with the Taoist sages. Thus it made possible the acceptance of Buddhism by the Chinese people, and led to the further transformation of the religion from India.

Are there not interesting inferences that Christians can make on this subject? We allude here to the need of furthering 'native' theologies, a need which the Buddhist encounter with Chinese 'religions' illustrates. We refer also to developments internal to Christian theology itself, to process theology for example, but also to liberation theology and to the general orientation of finding God in man. It is on this note that this paper concludes, with the wish that others further the intellectual dialogue hopefully begun.

Notes

1. See Julia Ching *Confucianism and Christianity* (Kodansha International 1977) ch. 1.

2. Ch'ien Tuan-sheng *The Government and Politics of China* (Cambridge 1950) p. 15.

3. See Needham *Science and Civilisation in China* (Cambridge 1956) pp. 2, 581, and Northrop *The Meeting of East and West* (Macmillan 1966) ch. 9-10.

4. Max Weber *The Religion of China* (Macmillan 1964) ch. 6.

5. Liang Su-ming *Tung-hsi wen-hua chi ch'i che-hsueh* (n.d.)

6. Hajime Nakamura *Ways of Thinking of Eastern Peoples* (1960).

7. James Legge *The Notions of the Chinese Concerning Gods and Spirits* (Hong Kong 1862, 1961 reprint) p. 24.

8. Evidence is provided by the *Book of Documents* and the *Book of Poetry*. See Julia Ching, op. cit. ch. 4.

9. Ruth Benedict *The Chrysanthemum and the Sword* (Riverside Press 1946) ch. 10. She speaks here especially of the Japanese, but what she says has frequently been extended to the Chinese.

10. Eberhard's book was published in 1967. Maspero's study of Taoism is included in his *Les Religions Chinoises*, vol. I, published posthumously (Paris 1967).

Michel Masson

Religious Roots and Implications of Maoism

INTRODUCTION

THE title of this article might suggest the following response: the religious implications of Maoism should be sought for in its double origin: the Chinese and the Marxist. Thus Maoism would be the original product of the meeting between China's ancient tradition and Marxism. At best Maoism would be the fulfilment of the Chinese tradition: the Marxist vision saving China from the deadweight of Confucianism, whereas Chinese tradition would save its Marxism from the dogmatisms of Leninism and Stalinism. At worst Maoism would be the continuation in Marxist language of the essentially political and areligious Chinese tradition: a moralising nationalism and State orthodoxy. Thus Maoism presents us with the same dilemma as that faced by our ancestors in the eighteenth century regarding Confucianism: Is it a superior manifestation of reason or an oriental despotism?

A response of this kind has the obvious advantage of attempting to situate Maoism in a global historical perspective. Instead of selecting certain Maoist themes which seem religious or anti-religious to us, we are invited to define the concept of 'religious' from the point of view of Chinese history. However, this response still presents problems.

For example is it true to say that Maoism is the 'original product of the meeting between China's ancient tradition and Marxist ideology'? I think it is important to stress here that Maoism is first and foremost the bringing of Marxism to the realities of twentieth-century China. This was conditioned by the needs of the revolution, political chance, and the psychology of the main protagonists. In all this there was not much

26

'encounter' with ancestral tradition—the revolution drove over tradition like a bulldozer. History was preserved, but only on condition that it said what people wanted it to say.

Moreover, 'Maoism' covers a multiplicity of phenomena. The word was coined at Harvard about a quarter of a century ago to designate the aspects of the Chinese revolution which did not conform to Marxist-Leninist orthodoxy, chiefly the role accorded to the peasant masses instead of the urban proletariat, in the takeover of power. However in China, there was especial stress on the military role and strategic genius of Mao himself. As the years went by Maoism expanded to include other themes: 'the great leap forward', the 'cultural revolution', 'the permanence of contradictions in socialist society' etc. Whereas the Chinese merely spoke of the 'thoughts of Mao Tse-tung', 'Maoism' became a philosophy in the West. Finally, studies such as Lucian Pye's have tried to react against an excessive preoccupation with the content of Mao's ideas, and offer a psycho-historical explanation of his personality.[1] In China itself, it looks as if a whole side of Maoism is going to be, for the time being at least, passed over in respectful silence.

Because of all these ambiguities, the proposition that Maoism is the original product of a meeting between Marxism and ancient Chinese tradition shows many weaknesses and it is too weak to bear the weight of our theological questions. I think, and I shall try to explain that (1) this weakness arises from the fact that Maoism cannot be an adequate object for our theological questions; and (2) the 'religious implications' in the meeting between Marxism and Chinese tradition are not to be found in the Maoist 'text', but rather in its 'context': the intellectual and religious crisis of China in the twentieth century.

THE DIFFICULTY IN ASKING RELIGIOUS QUESTIONS ABOUT MAOISM

1. The Maoist experience

Recent studies have tried to discover whether Maoist ethics are practised with the fervour suggested in certain quarters. For example, Richard Madsen examined the behaviour of cadres in a village in the Canton region during the years 1964-1971.[2] How far do these cadres support, reinterpret, or even betray the Maoist vision? What social forces are at work in the village encouraging them to accept or reject the Maoist vision?

This study shows that the Maoist 'vision' functions as a political ideology, that is to say it is a trump card in the game of political power. There are other trump cards, some as un-Maoist as family relationships or social standing, but nothing is possible without a minimum of conformity to the externals of Maoism. Apart from this political game, the vision has little function. There are plenty of idealists but this is because political fervour is the only trump card they still hold to try to rehabilitate themselves politically. Thus the Canton school students who chose to come and live in the village in 1964 did so because they thought that this would be a way of getting the sins of their parents forgiven. They failed. The village cadres and the central government were not interested in Maoist purity but in conformity.

Thus Marxism as it is lived is a formal consensus, an instrument of political manipulation. Perhaps this is inevitable but this makes it difficult to assess the experience of Maoism religiously . . . except as an *emptiness*. According to other analysts, people who wake up one day to find they have become victims of the system realise that they have been caught in the vicious circle of hatred and begin to ask questions about the meaning of life. An event such as the earthquake at T'angshan (July 1976) made people ask religious questions.[3] Thus at the level of experience, the 'religious' seems as if it is to be found *outside* Maoism and often against it.

2. *Maoist thought*

But what about the religious implications of the thoughts of Mao? First we must mention certain questions about the status of these 'thoughts'.

Firstly, granted Mao's historical greatness, it still remains to be asked whether his *thoughts* were as important as his *actions*. This is doubtful. His personality, his political acumen and historical accident explain his success just as well or better than his thoughts. Furthermore, his thoughts are not a system transcending the different particular situations of his career. If a certain theme reappears ten years later in another political context, it is given a different meaning. We cannot treat his thoughts as a 'body of work' without constant reference to Mao's political biography.

So should our theological inquiry be directed towards Mao's thoughts, or should it not be towards the *lasting results of his actions*? Among these results, Benjamin Schwartz has recently mentioned the restoration of national dignity, the egalitarian distribution of resources, the importance given to agriculture and the awareness that China must discover her own road to modernisation. On the other hand the same writer asks whether the great inspiring themes of constant struggle and the march forward— the Long March constantly appearing in Mao's poems—are not really secondary. After all, Schwartz says, the masses also know that there are many aspects of human life missing from the great Maoist fresco of history.[4]

Finally we must remember that Mao's 'thoughts' have the ambiguous virtue of having *silenced* all other thinkers, both Marxist and non-Marxist. This is remarkable. What is also remarkable is the recent publication in China of a forgotten speech by Mao in which he said he was not infallible.

These points, among others, caution the theologian trying to ask questions about Mao's thoughts. Theresa Chu has recently given an example of this caution in a study called 'The Religious Dimension in the Thought of Mao Tse-tung'.[5] Her method consists in formalising Mao's thoughts by using Paul Tillich's categories: Does Mao's text go beyond the utilitarian, is it open to transcendence, essential in all religion? With this interpretative framework, Th. Chu shows us a Mao preoccupied with the question of Being in his total submission to the movement of history. He is neither a pure pragmatist nor a utopian, but grasps the essential link between technology and humanisation, the dialectical movement to be fulfilled in history but which is directed to something beyond history.

This religious dimension is 'authentic', says Th. Chu, because it is in touch with the living sources of Chinese history at the very moment in which China faces the demands of the present. Mao breaks the chains of false orthodoxies, both those of Confucianism and those of liberalism and Moscow dogmatism. Thus he is free to rediscover the 'originally true' at the same time responding to the needs of the historical present with technologisation and humanisation.

The author explains clearly that what she is examining is neither Mao's practice nor the specific content of his thoughts. Her reading is 'formal', using categories which are not Mao's. She attempts to deduce from Mao's texts how he would deal with our own categories: to construct in some manner what is *not said* about religion in Mao's text.

Her method is rigorously defined and in this it is exemplary. However, one wonders whether Tillich's categories, even if they are applicable to all religions, are also applicable to a text which is not purporting to be a religious text. At best, it seems to me, Th. Chu's thesis would amount to the fact that: if one day Maoism became the religious language of China, Mao's text could be interpreted in the Tillichian categories of the 'religious'.

Thus Th. Chu's research seems to confirm the difficulty of asking religious questions about Maoism, because Maoism does not intend to be religious and is the unfinished text of a revolution in progress.

We conclude that we do not have to give up asking our questions, but that the theologian must destroy the illusion of a 'Maoist thought' encased in sacred isolation. We can only study Maoism in the context of the whole crisis of Chinese consciousness in the twentieth century. We must abandon the exotic fascination of a work of genius produced by Mao alone, and remember all the other thinkers, even Marxist ones, who were silenced. The theologian should spend more time studying the intellectual history of China before 1949, and try to discover the religious themes inherent in the modernisation. He should try to discern the 'religious implications' of the economic and socio-political crisis in which Mao intervened. I will try to give a brief survey of these implications in what follows.

RELIGIOUS IMPLICATIONS: UNIVERSAL LAWS AND INTRACTABLE PARTICULARITY

In China, like everywhere else, modernisation brings with it a religious crisis. The crisis arises from the conflict between a traditional vision and a new vision, with new values, chiefly derived from the development of Western science. The question is to define how this universal conflict affected China in particular.

Firstly we note that in China the crisis came before modernisation. In the nineteenth century China was confronted with a modern world with new technologies and ideologies. Industrialisation was a cultural problem before it became a reality. The phenomenon was reinforced by the absence of distinctions between different branches of knowledge, between the politician and the philosopher, and on a wider scale between the nation and the cultural community.

A well-known symptom of this crisis was the attack on tradition led by Mao's generation from 1915 onwards. This iconoclasm was not caused only by political disappointments, but was a sign of a crisis of consciousness which Lin Yu-sheng attributes to *three factors*.

First there was the disappearance in 1911-12 of the figure of the Emperor. He exercised universal kingship. By virtue of a quasi-sacramental charisma he embodied and signified the union between the divine and the human, the political and the cultural. Thus his disappearance was an event as tragic as the death of God for Nietzsche.

The second factor was this generation's inability to distinguish the social norms or practical policies which they opposed with cultural symbols and traditional values. In other words the integration of the socio-political order and the culture in the person of the Emperor had been reflected in people's attitudes for centuries. In 1911 the symbol broke but people continued to think in terms of integration; the intellectuals sought another total system to replace it and found it in Darwinism, scientism, Marxism.

The third factor was what Lin Yu-sheng called a culturo-intellectualist attitude: the belief that cultural and intellectual transformation should precede economic and social change. This idealism had Neo-Confucian roots: the Empire was a moral substance; the mastery of the classics was the essential preparation for public service. After the break in 1911 there was a split between moral fervour and objective socio-economic laws.[6]

Thus this analysis describes a world which had lost its language of unity, for which Marxism offered a new integration. It is in this context that we can grasp the double origin of Chinese Marxism: not Marx and Lenin meeting Confucius and Lao Tzu but Chinese intellectuals finding in Marx in 1920 an answer to the particular problems of their generation.

Seeking a new integrating vision in objective laws they quickly realised that these 'universal laws' were difficult to apply to Chinese history. Faith in a universal explanation opened the doors on the Chinese past. This question of the meaning of history is also a religious question: it asks whether Chinese experience has a vision of man and the universe, a 'spirit', something 'irreducible'. It also asks whether this irreducible element still has a place in a world explained by universal laws.

This tension between universal laws and intractable particularity is central to the philosophical debates in the period before 1949. In these debates it was agreed that in the Chinese experience this irreducible element was not confined to religion, but to the philosophical and cultural tradition: *the experience of transcendence was not enclosed within the religious.* Having said this they then had to define this tradition.

One of the chief protagonists, Fung Yu-lan, thought that the crisis was not dramatic: it was no more than the transition from a rural world to an industrial society. By using a technological explanation of history, which he called Marxist, Fung claimed that 'Chinese' values were no different from those of any other pre-industrial society. As for Chinese philosophy, it had nothing irreducible about it. It was the product of a mono-cultural and pre-scientific world. Thus it needed to be reinterpreted on the lines that Fung in the twentieth century could finally give philosophy, with the benefit of Marx, Russell and Wittgenstein.[7]

Thus Fung attempted to eliminate all signs of intractable particularity. He was accused of 'breaking down the faith' by other Neo-Confucians who supported an irreducible Chinese experience which couldn't be grasped or interpreted except from the inside. For this group, Ho Lin explained, philosophy was a 'concrete force' capable of creating cultures.[8] Against Fung's philosophical detachment we find a 'language of faith', full of religious fervour for tradition.

What was really at stake in this debate was analysed by Liang Sou-ming in a book finished in 1949. For Liang, the claim to intractable particularity led to a dramatic clarity. China had followed its own way, explained Liang, but for several centuries it had no longer been a road but a dead-end. Spiritually, economically and politically, China was sick. Chinese vision, the idea of a cultural community governed by moral reason, had been perverted. China was 'trapped' by its own history: it was an essentially rural and disorganised society, needing to seek long and diligently its own way of modernising, both economically and spiritually.[9]

Of course the religious crisis was not confined to what was said by these few thinkers, but the question they asked remains to be answered.[10] The question of an intractable particularity which could not survive confrontation with 'universal' laws and truths, or if they were not universal, at least imported. It remains to be seen if one day the 'meeting' of Marxism with Chinese tradition will happen and if an 'original product' will emerge in the sphere of religious vision. Moreover, a religious 'image' is perhaps more important than the pre-1949 Neo-Confucians thought. In order to penetrate Maoist or post-Maoist conformism and rediscover Chinese tradition, perhaps something more is needed than contemporary Neo-Confucianism. Something like the 'image' of Buddha or Christ? The question remains to be answered and time will show.

Translated by Dinah Livingstone

Notes

1. L. Pye *Mao Tse-tung: The Man in the Leader* (New York 1976).

2. R. Madsen 'Revolutionary Asceticism in Communist China: Social Causes and Consequences of Commitment to the Maoist Ethics in a South China Village', Doctoral Thesis (Harvard University 1977).

3. M. and I. D. London 'Christ in China' *Worldview* 21:4 (1978).

4. B. I. Schwartz in *Mao Tse-tung in the Scales of History* D. Wilson (ed.) (London 1977) pp. 9-34.

5. Th. Chu 'The Religious Dimension in Mao Tse-tung's Thought' *Theology Annual* (Hong Kong) 2 (1978). This article is part of a doctoral thesis in theology for the University of Chicago, 1977.

6. Lin Yü-sheng in *Reflections on the May Fourth Movement* B. I. Schwartz (ed.) (Cambridge, Mass. 1972) pp. 27-29.

7. Feng Yu-lan *Hsin Shih-lun* (Kunming 1940); *Hsin Chih-yen* (Shanghai 1946); *The Spirit of Chinese Philosophy* (London 1947).

8. Ho Lin *Tang tai Chung-kuo che-hsueh* (Hong Kong 1963).

9. Liang Sou-ming *Chung-kuo wen-hua yao-i* (Hong Kong 1963).

10. For a fuller description of the crisis see Chan Wing-tsit *Religious Trends in Modern China* (New York 1953).

Hung Chih

Chinese Daily Life as a
Locus for Ethics

THIS essay takes as its subject matter daily life as it is lived in the People's Republic of China and treats it from an ethical viewpoint. Such an undertaking involves (1) a description of the tone, quality and character of the life in question; and (2) an assessment of its underlying value system as well as a clarification of the stance from which the assessment is made.

One might object to the term 'Chinese daily life' on the ground that there are 900 million Chinese living in vastly different climates and occupied with totally different kinds of work. One might also raise the question as to the particular period in which the Chinese way of life is described. A third question might be raised concerning the sources of the description.

First of all, the description is not aimed at specific customs which may differ from place to place although specifics must serve as the basis of description. Diversity notwithstanding, there seems to be enough in common in the lives of the Chinese people to make the treatment of the topic possible.

Secondly, by 'Chinese daily life' is meant that which is observable to date. Present-day China cannot be explained out of the context of its past. How China has kept its identity is another question, but life today has decidedly taken on a new dimension, and it is precisely this newness that will be the focus of this essay.

As to the sources used, the writer's first hand observations, travellers' notes, emigrants' reports, news media and Chinese publications all form part of the resource material. Possibly all these put together do not inform us of all the aspects of life in China. But with Clifford Geertz, we think

33

that 'it is not necessary to know everything in order to understand something'.[1]

The task of an interpreter, then, is to make sense out of some salient features observed, to grasp intuitively the hopes and longings of a people, to share with them their convictions as well as their own awareness of what needs to be done. By penetrating into a people's way of life, the interpreter hopes to gain insight into its underlying value system. It is hoped that the assessment which follows will be the voice of conscience of the people themselves rather than an alien voice.

ATTITUDE OF CARE

For someone going to China from a consumption-oriented society, the country seems like a different world indeed. There is a limited number of goods available, although recently a relative increase in this respect has been noted. There are no commercial advertisements and wastage is minimal. Whether one travels by air or by train, is at someone's home or in the streets, one is struck by an overwhelmingly simple life-style.

This simplicity is accompanied by an attitude of care in treating material things. In the social atmosphere thus created, the traveller is reminded of the sacred character of the universe in which he or she lives. Although the simple life-style can be attributed to the scarcity of resources at the disposal of the individual and/or nation as a whole, scarcity alone would not result in life being lived as it is in the People's Republic. For one thing, scarcity does not bring fear. On the contrary, it is softened, as it were, by a strong sense of security which is the outcome of the fact that people's basic needs are cared for.

A little boy of seven received the gift of a small bag of candies which he loved. He left it on his table. Two weeks later it was still in the same place. When asked why the candies had not yet disappeared, he answered, 'I eat one each day'. A child who would do this while living in abject poverty might draw pity. But this boy is one of the many happy, healthy-looking children one sees in streets, parks, nurseries and schools. Against such a background, the behaviour of that little boy perhaps exemplifies a rational approach to the problem of scarcity.

A child who saves his candies still acts out of common sense. But an adult who treats things with care may do so from a different perspective. This seems to be the case for a great majority of people. Their attitude towards *things* has risen out of a changed consciousness. It is the consciousness of those who are convinced that sharing is fair. With this conviction, a dimension of meaning has entered into daily life qualifying it and giving it a unique character. The care that manifests itself is the care of a free person, not that of a slave to nature.

Another effect of changed consciousness can be seen in the care people have for one another. In this respect, China provides another kind of security which invigorates the young and brings comfort to the aged and the sick.

An eighty-two-year-old man convalescing at home received visits from friendly neighbours as well as the cadre of the neighbourhood committee. A sixty-three-year-old woman in bad health and without relatives near by was accompanied by neighbours to the bus stop each time she wanted to go out. Neighbours also visited her and shopped for her. A twenty-year-old beginner in an accounting department felt encouraged because his senior colleague helped him locate a penny mistake in the balance sheet. A teacher in her thirties was touched by her colleagues who volunteered to replace her in some of her duties so that she could spend more time with a sick child. These examples can be multiplied and they are by no means unique to China. What makes them special is perhaps the fact that they are practised by an awakened people.

The Chinese Revolution meant war against the Nationalist army, struggles against big landlords and capitalists, rich peasants, supporters of imperialists, and others who opposed the revolution. It also meant a united front among industrial workers, richer and poorer peasants, intellectuals except those who associated with the enemy, all labouring people, the destitute, and the left-wing of the national bourgeoisie. In defining the enemies and the friends of the working class, Mao Tse-tung used three criteria: relationship with imperialists, ownership of means of production, and attitude towards the revolution.[2] As a result, many who owned some means of production were still included among the allies of the working class and in the course of the past thirty years, it was possible for them too to acquire a new outlook on life.

Thus many have come to realise that massive suffering existed in China because of the old social structures. The term 'class enemy' may mean nothing to people outside China, but to the Chinese it means structural evil as well as the enemy within their own hearts. The effort to change the structures in order to bring human dignity to an overwhelming majority has resulted in a sense of mutuality making the relationship among the people qualitatively different.

Whereas in any country of the world including China, people are motivated to help one another by charity, compassion and/or guilt, the awareness of structural evil has lessened the importance of such motivations in China. It has been recognised that peasants and workers would have been better teachers or physicians had they been given the same training as the latter. Those who have more still help those who have less, but it is no longer 'good' individuals performing good deeds. Doing good has been de-privatised, so to speak. There has been a socialisation of human relations which provides deep security to people living in China.

TRANSFORMATION OF THE PERSON

The above described character of life in China involves an internalisation of values such as sharing and caring. China has been noted for its emphasis on values and attitudes; through education, the young are being taught socialist values. But as has been indicated above, the caring attitude for some at least is rooted in a new awareness rather than in the desire to conform to a social behavioural pattern. The new ethos is inseparable from the new worldview which has been the gift of the revolution to many. Given the fact that the new ethos has emerged in the relatively recent past, the process of transformation is still fresh in the memory of the people concerned. By reviewing some peak moments in this process, perhaps further light can be thrown on the dominant character of Chinese society today.

For some, the transformation process began with a shock. Upon Liberation, they were shown a small factory in Shanghai where workers, all teenagers, were so disfigured by poisonous gas that they no longer had any sense of smell. Yet they had to continue working in the same factory for want of an alternative.

Another kind of shock came in the reformatory for Shanghai's thousands of prostitutes. Those who had a part to play in the reforming process were deeply struck when they assisted at parent-daughter interviews where hundreds of parents—either from the countryside or from the city slums—told their respective daughters how they resorted to selling them to white slave traders because of poverty.

These sessions were powerful because of the truth they revealed. And the truth, according to one person present, was that the prostitutes were born like everybody else, and that it was circumstances which made such tragedies possible. Subsequent events proved this, since, with the exception of a handful, these prostitutes have been rehabilitated and re-integrated into society.

To be exposed to the darker side of the old society brought the awareness that no partial solution could adequately deal with problems such as prostitution and child labour. The power of money enabled those who have it to control the market in such a way that they could make more money. At the same time, they themselves are controlled by money since the profit motive dominates them, and through it, other lives as well. In the examples given above, teenagers were not only selling their labour power but their physical beings as well. The actual remedy brought to these problems convinced many that a radical change was needed in China.

But this was only one aspect of the transformative process. Another aspect touched the heart of the person involved. It consisted in a new insight into one's being. In the light of the discovery that the prostitutes were innocent and the teenage workers were promising youths, the self-image of the person changed. His/her former self-righteousness disappeared and along with it, the understanding of the human person as an atomistic individual. This experience was not just an intellectual understanding of the structural roots of social problems as mentioned above, it was symptomatic of a transformation of the whole person.

Those who have undergone such processes seemed to have come in touch with truth and justice. For split seconds perhaps, their individual beings merged with society as a whole. A new horizon opened for them. Old myths broke and old categories burst. Later, they may again return to an atomistic mode of being, but even then, their life is not likely to be the same as before. The discovery of meaning that came with the experience freed the person from former inhibitions. All the important categories in public life began to have their previous underlying assumptions questioned.

In medicine, for example, the assumption was no longer held that the doctor was all powerful or that Western medicine alone was efficacious. In education, it was no longer taken for granted that the teacher knew everything. Politics in China used to mean power, command, and paternalism. Today, it means service. In literature and art, the principle of art for art's sake was questioned. These are but a few examples of how Chinese culture in its various aspects was shaken at its foundations and how new growth came out of ancient roots. In the light of the transformative experience described above, meaning is understood in terms of the whole rather than the parts. The more one views agriculture and industry, manual work and intellectual work, leaders and led, physicians and patient, teacher and student as opposites that essentially belong together, the more one recognises their separation from each other in actual life. The emphasis on the actual state of contradiction in each of the sets of opposites presupposes an understanding of their essential dependence on each other.

The Cultural Revolution from 1966 to 1976, especially its first two years, represented a massive effort to embody the new ethos. It had the boldness and the temerity to effect changes hitherto considered unthinkable: selection of candidates for universities by peasants and workers, obligatory manual work for professors and students, economics put under the command of politics, to name but a few.

Since October 1976, however, many policies of the period have been changed. The institutions then created have been modified if not eliminated. The 'Four Modernisations' of agriculture, industry, science and technology, and defence have been defined as the goal of the current period. Economics is now in command. University students are selected on the basis of a unified entrance exam. Manual work for intellectuals, if done, is not to exceed one-sixth of their working time. The question arises as to why such major changes so soon. What do the changes mean? What is the future prospect? In considering these questions, the relationship between worldview and policies will be discussed and the normative question will also come into play.

THE NORMATIVE QUESTION

According to the new worldview described above, the universe is no longer seen as a static entity, for such a view would lead to a valuation of unchangeable principles. Obviously if norms of the old society had been taken as absolutes, there would not have been a revolution. For the moment at least, the shattering of the old universe seems to correspond to the discovery of a living reality. Truth and justice discovered within the Chinese situation and not through a process of abstraction had liberated the human being pre-disposed towards the true and the just. Not only did a new ethos arise, but also new policies were sparked off in the gigantic task of building a socialist China. We suggested above that many policies made during the first two years of the Cultural Revolution were congruous with the new ethos. The fact that they have been changed after a relatively short period seems to justify the claim that these policies have failed.

The search for a basic explanation involves a re-examination of the worldview which served as the inspirational source of the policies in question. For, although a particular worldview is not necessarily linked with one set of policies, certain policies may reflect latent contradictions within the worldview supporting it. This is not to minimise the importance of external factors which may have shortened the life-span of these policies. Political scientists and historians will come to our help with their analyses of those factors. But as Mao said, '. . . external causes are the condition of change and internal causes are the basis of change, . . . external causes become operative through internal causes'.[3]

What, then, is that intrinsic cause? Charles Bettelheim attributes the failure of Cultural Revolution policies to the absence of an up-to-date class analysis.[4] He points out that Mao's analysis made in 1926 no longer applied and that a class struggle waged without a scientific analysis opens the door to abuses. That such abuses did take place is supported by materials recently released from China. There were ill-founded arrests and criticisms of Party members as well as of others. In many cases, debates ended in fighting, injury or death. The disillusionment of patriotic people in this experience reflects the difficulty of finding suitable criteria in the criticism campaign.

By 1966, many former bourgeois elements—not to mention Party members—had undergone a radical change in worldview. Not only had they accepted the leadership of the Communist Party, but also they had been serving the people with enthusiasm under that leadership. The question of criteria became all the more crucial because the Cultural Revolution was intended to be 'a great revolution that touches people to their very souls'.[5] The way the Chinese Revolution emphasised ideology opened the vista of grassroots individuals to a total humanity. It represented the greatest strength of the revolution. Its power penetrated into the very 'souls' of a numerous people. The same, however, became its greatest weakness as the difficulties encountered during the Cultural Revolution have shown.

One might wonder 'Why the Cultural Revolution at all?' The answer to this question leads further towards an understanding of the worldview in question. For that worldview is essentially non-codifiable. It was not reducible to any dogma—Marxism, Leninism or Mao Tse-tung's Thought. This meant a relativisation of previous values. The experience of personal transformation described above testifies to the non-dogmatic approach to creeds in the years following Liberation. During the first years of the Cultural Revolution, new policies were marked by the same flexibility, it seems. Yet as time went on, those who implemented the policies under the leadership of the so-called 'Gang of Four' became dogmatists. Flexibility was undermined. The explicit purpose of the Cultural Revolution was only partly realised since the actual effect on the minds and hearts of a portion of patriotic individuals became binding rather than liberating.

The problem faced by the Gang of Four is a basic problem for all good-willed people. The rhythm of life demands moments of affirmation as well as moments of negation. To leave oneself free for the summons of human nature, one must continually negate the claim of all human creations and institutions, no matter how good, to be absolute. Yet no one can live on negations alone. How not to absolutise that which is humanly good is perhaps the final test of earnest supporters of the 'good of the people'. Whatever is done in the name of the people must then have an opening towards further change. Revolutionary ethics chooses policies, but it must be ready for criticism and self-criticism at any point in history. That seems to be the closest one can come to a 'norm' on the grounds of justice for all people. That norm is a mode of being which brings with it a healthy atmosphere in which to live, and that atmosphere is a public thing since life itself is both public and private.

In the light of the above considerations, during the past few years China has made a gigantic step forward in liberating people's minds from dogmatism. However, the programme of modernisation is not without its risks. To emphasise science and technology is not only justifiable, but good and necessary. It is one thing to make this emphasis, and quite another to assume that means used in a socialist society *automatically* lead to socialist ends. Past history has shown that results of means chosen do not always match declared ends. Regardless of differences within, the Chinese Communist Party has been proud of its past accomplishments in transforming people and in creating a new ethos. To continue in the spirit of the historical changes which the revolution has brought about, the memory of class struggle must be kept, it seems, not only as a thing of the past, but also as part of the present mode of being.

One young teacher in China tells of her experience in 1964 when she went to the countryside. According to her, that experience changed her. The fact that it was Liu Shao-chi's wife—one who was severely criticised during the Cultural Revolution—who sent her there did not matter. The change that took place in her was real. This teacher represents, it seems, one locus where the memory of class struggle will be kept.

On another level, signs of such memory can be found in the way the modernisers are leading China. The present leadership criticises the way the Gang of Four indiscriminately labelled people as 'capitalist-roaders'. In its approach to the evaluation of the ten years of the Cultural Revolution, it is pointing out the positive as well as the negative elements. While showing that production suffered under the Gang of Four, news media in China have also given statistical proofs of steady increases in production in certain localities during the same years. In new ways, the great experiment of Chinese socialism involving the whole human being will continue, hopefully, in order to bring about yet greater meaning in the lives of the Chinese people.

In the past experience of the Chinese Revolution, the transformation of the person coincided with a shifting of focus to the larger community including all classes of people: peasants, workers, army, cadre, intellectuals and others. Success in the future will perhaps also depend on the active involvement of all. 'Class struggle' in China has taken on a dimension of depth, but the world has not yet found any suitable category to embody that dimension. One can only hope that in the case of China, progress made in the realm of science and technology will continue to touch the very souls of the people. For that will be the best sign of a healthy society.

Notes

1. Clifford Geertz *The Interpretation of Cultures* (New York 1973) p. 20.

2. Mao Tse-tung *Selected Works* Vol. I (Peking 1967) pp. 13-19.

3. Ibid. p. 314.

4. Charles Bettelheim 'The great leap backward' *Monthly Review* XXX-3 pp. 93 ff.

5. *Decision of the Chinese Communist Party Central Committee Concerning the Great Cultural Revolution* Aug. 8, 1966, in A. Doak Barnett *China after Mao* (Princeton 1967) p. 263.

Claude Larré

The Meaning of Transcendence
in Chinese Thought

THE Chinese represent one of the finest strains of the human species. Yet however gifted they may be from many points of view, they are nevertheless revealed to be temperamentally areligious. Some people attribute this to race, others, more numerous, to a culturally acquired abnormality —an abnormality which serves to explain the fact that China has been in no hurry to respond in a positive way to the repeated advances of Christianity. The view I have just outlined—without making it my own—has a long history and still persists in the minds of many people. Without being flippant, I would like to recall a scene from *Le Soulier de Satin* which illustrates the aptitude of the Chinese for getting to the heart of things and not allowing themselves to be deceived. The action is between a converter of souls and his Chinese servant. The poor devil has just learned that he possesses a soul and that this object is something unique and of great value. An interminable haggling session immediately ensues, from which sordid and bizarre exchange I recall this one sound observation: that it takes time for a man, who is occupied day and night seeking the means of survival, to grasp the fact that he has a soul and to appreciate it at its true worth. I also think that in the 'souls trade' supply only meets demand when it is in a position to elicit it. It could be that the Chinese do not have time to be religious in the way it seems we are ourselves; but it could also be that their demand is not orientated towards our supply. There is surely a good deal of arrogance and not a little hypocrisy in the judgments that have been made about their so-called religious inadequacy.

I will begin here by outlining two arguments, one of which is exaggeratedly negative, while the other exaggerates the sensibility of the

Chinese to religious realities; I will indicate the element of truth that can nevertheless be discerned in the one and the other; and finally I will show briefly the importance of the Taoist spiritual tradition for a possible proclamation of the Revelation of God that has come to us in Jesus Christ—though I have no intention of suggesting that the Taoist Way is to be preferred to the Confucian way; it is simply that in a short article one cannot hope to cover every aspect of a subject of this kind.

CRITICAL

The thesis which I have labelled negative is to be found among people who have a lifelong acquaintance with the Chinese and who have tasted all the bitterness of misunderstanding, indifference or rejection. It was formulated during the period when relations between the Church and China were at their worst: at the time of the Controversy of Rites.[1]

The Chinese, the argument goes, adore their ancestors. They practise an idolatrous cult of Confucius and other cultural heroes, and through the ministry of the Emperor, whose person is sacred, they offer to Heaven the worship they deny to the true God. As for the people, they take themselves off to the innumerable temples that are to be found in the towns and villages and there they carry out their devotions before the Emperor of Jade, a more familiar and accessible substitute for Heaven. Every moment of life, from that of conception to that of death and burial, is wrapped round with a tissue of superstitions. The liturgies celebrated by the Buddhist monks and Taoist priests, both in the temples and in the houses of private individuals, the calendar of pagan feasts, and the most extravagant forms of divination all bear witness to the piety of the Chinese which is used to serve their material interests through a total distortion of genuine religious spirit.

This unflattering picture is now old and out of date. Even allowing for the truth of a number of the points it makes, does it prove that the Chinese are naturally or culturally incapable of genuine religious feeling? Is it based on a faulty evaluation which has very little that is Christian about it and which I will describe as idealist. Christians are not, in fact, idealists; they are disciples of the Incarnation. But incarnation is the very charism that is proper to China. Her people are an enduring, active and resourceful race of men, skilful, practical, quick to grasp the essential qualities of things and to make use of the opportune moment when it comes, and whose capacity for living is remarkable. Once they were known as the Heavenly Ones, and later they were to come to be known as the Earthly Ones. Does all this make them incapable of ever thinking of God in a way that is worthy of him?

COMPLIMENTARY

Having recalled, no doubt with a certain degree of exaggeration, the negative position of those who conclude rather hastily, though not without some apparent justification, that the Chinese are lacking in religious sense, I must, to be fair, mention the contrary position which, considered from a strictly Christian point of view, does, in my opinion, a still greater disservice to the reputation of the Chinese. It is commonly found in unqualified admirers of Chinese wisdom, and eighteenth-century Europe, following the *philosophes*, who were French more often than not, fell into this bizarre line of thinking. We should admire the wisdom of a people who are content to organise man's journey through this world on a basis of law and moral education, entrusting the task of educating their children and the responsibility for administering their towns to men chosen from the world of philosophy and letters. The latter respect the opinions and beliefs of all, though they themselves adhere to none but those they have met with in their ancient books. They practise tolerance all the better for seeking to understand man only from the natural point of view. Their idea of God, whom they call Heaven, is at once sublime and very general. They set a high value on moral rectitude and very little on the details of religious practice.

Here is a very clear description of a Chinese religion not overconcerned about religious feeling. You will not find it anywhere in the form in which I have just presented it, yet it is the deism of the Chinese as it might have been imagined in Paris during the eighteenth century. Going beyond what various memoirs and descriptions and the correspondence of the Jesuits of the Peking mission have to say about the 'religion' of the Chinese and the mentality of the scholars, the *philosophes* used the information to attack the despotism of the monarchy and the obscurantism of the Church. All the insights which reached them from the distant Empire of China they made part of the 'Enlightenment'.

I would summarise the above by saying that generalities, whether sympathetic or hostile, about the Chinese, have a long history. I only mentioned them in order to be able now to set them on one side, and because they still constitute a preliminary obstacle to understanding of the spirit and religious attitude of the Chinese.

CHINESE CHRISTIAN SCHOLARS

Rather than remain in the company of Westerners in our efforts to appreciate the Chinese, let us instead turn to those Chinese Christians who have a personal experience of Jesus Christ and a personal knowledge of their own people; who—and this is very important—remain attached to their traditional culture while opening themselves to the rest of the world. What do these men have to say who read the *Book of Odes* in the original, searching there for signs of God's presence, who put the *Book of Changes* into practice and ponder in the light of it the incessant shift in the balance of those forces which make and remake the temporal structure of the world, who meditate on Chinese history and discover within it models for the more universal history of human groups? These men who commune with Confucius and Mencius, always present for them, who weep for joy with Meiti when he announces that the time has come to renew such feudal elements as there are in Confucius by passing them through the fire of universal love? These men who, appalled by the iron rigidity of the lawmakers' pronouncements, recognise that anarchy and hypocrisy are latent in every society of inordinate size? Men who are enthralled when they hear Lao Tzu and Chuang Tzu recalling that the dust from which man was formed is a cosmic dust, kindled into life by a fire which will never go out, and that herein lies the problem of problems: that of the survival of the ephemeral in the incessant cycle of cosmic birth and rebirth? Men who find, transposed, in a landscape, a painting, a piece of porcelain or a symphony the ultimate questions about the destiny of each one of us? These minds, whose boundless culture is enlarged by the particular cultures which their knowledge of Western languages makes it possible for them to appreciate from the inside? These men for whom the human being is never anything but a particular instance of the earth's power to produce, made fruitful by the grace of Heaven which determines an individual destiny for each one of us? What precisely have they to say when, with all the strength they derive from the Confucian ethic and the freedom Taoist spirituality gives them, they hear themselves being described as incompetent in religious matters?

I would not advise anyone to tell them that 'the absence of any sense of the transcendence of God and the vagueness of a notion of God which does not allow one to establish a personal relationship with him serve to explain the manifest obstacle that stands in the way of dialogue between Christianity and China'. To prove that I am right I will cite a statement made by Dr John Wu, which was recalled by his lifelong friend and companion, Professor Paul Sih.[2] It is a reminder that Confucianism and Taoism offer a contrasted approach to the mystery of man, before God, in an authentic relationship, in spirit and in truth.

Dr Wu began by quoting two verses from Psalm 96 (7):

Cloud and darkness surround him (Yahweh),
Righteousness and justice support his throne;

and then, drawing on all the resources of one who has lived his conversion to Jesus Christ throughout his life, he goes on to comment on them: 'Confucianism taught me to appreciate the second proposition, Taoism the first. But it was Catholicism that enabled me to understand the text as a whole.' What John Wu said there he has said elsewhere, in almost every one of his works.[3] John Wu thinks like that, and all Chinese intellectuals think in the same way. The concept of power, of God at work in every spiritual man—and obviously I do not exclude non-Christians—is perhaps all that is needed to help us rediscover in Confucianism the sense of moral transcendence with which Confucius himself was imbued, and to make the mystical sense which underlies the writings of men like the author of *The Book of the Way and of Virtue* shine forth from Taoism.[4] More generally speaking, all Chinese who lived from Heaven were followers of the way of Transcendence and were embarked, as their lives frequently show, on a spiritual path. In the last analysis, is it the reality of the religious life of the Chinese that interests us, or are we concerned with the futile exercise of looking to them for theological doctrines, which are obviously worthy of respect but characterised historically by an intellectual activity as yet unable to attach any importance to theirs? There is no point in expecting the Chinese, who are steeped in a civilisation which only came lately to knowledge of Christianity, to have the same ideas and aspirations regarding God's transcendence *vis-à-vis* man and the world as the Western Christian. Instead one should ask of the Chinese what Plato asked for: that they should seek the Truth with all their heart. As long as they do not regard themselves as persons, how can one expect them to have a personal relationship with Jesus Christ, with God? The idea that God is a person and, as such, the ground of the existence of human persons may be a reflection of man's aspirations; it is certainly not one of the data of natural religion!

CONFUCIAN TRANSCENDENCE

I am leaving aside for the time being examination of the Confucianism of Confucius and Mencius, which alludes with great delicacy to the role of Heaven in the government of the universe and its presence within man and to the effort that is required before man's conscience can return to its state of original purity, and so reflect the divine light. It establishes the norms of behaviour that man must follow in order to discover within his own depths the mainspring of justice, in the biblical sense of the term, and the rules for life in society which are given concrete form in rites and ceremonies, although their source is within. On the basis of all this one can say that for Confucius, and *before* Confucius, there existed in China a religious dimension which was responsive to the divine transcencence as the basis of personal spirituality and transcendental morality.

Having said briefly what I wanted to say about the merits of the Confucianism of the time of Confucius and the good that I find in it, I come now to Taoist mysticism, which, in the minds of the educated Chinese, is simply another approach to the Way of Heaven.

TRANSCENDENCE OF THE WAY AND OF VIRTUE

The position I would like to defend can be outlined as follows:

The Chinese possess in Taoism a conception of the Way of Heaven as absolutely transcendent and radically immanent. The Way of the Taoists is the Way of Heaven. To define it specifically as the 'Way of Heaven' is to distinguish it from the thousand and one other ways which are the paths traced out by the comings and goings of men. The Way is made manifest through its Virtue. The Way and its Virtue is the manifestation of the invisible Reality; Reality as one can perceive it and affirm it while one is a being-in-this-world. It constitutes the rule for action, and at the same time it is the mysterious movement of 'Return' of what is temporarily dispersed in ten thousand beings. The Way is transcendent, inscrutable, ineffable . . . but its transcendence is not an obstacle to intimacy with it. Man's relationship to the Way is that of a nursling to its mother, and he enjoys with it an intimacy which is all the more genuine in that the distinctions proper to the state of conscious awareness disappear in an unconscious awareness which one would be wrong to describe as an inferior state of awareness. As the Taoist writings are regarded as pantheistic and monistic by many authors, I feel bound to defend them against this accusation. I would argue that the great early Taoist writings are neither monistic nor pantheistic when one reads and understands them with the mentality of those who wrote them, and I would take as an example a few lines from chapter VI of the work of Chuang Tzu, a text that is more reliable and more approachable than others. The title of chapter VI reads as follows:

'Great Ancestor, our Master'
The Way: life that is overflowing, yet faithful; non-action on the part of the non-visible; all-pervading and elusive, that one may possess but not see; its stem is its own, and its root; before Heaven-and-Earth came

to be it subsists, always and forever. Spirits of the lower world and sovereign spirits, it is from the Way that the one and the other derive their spirituality. Creator of Heaven, Creator of the Earth, but existing outside time. It can be traced back to the furthest Antiquity and yet is ageless.

Commentary: The Way manifests itself as overflowing with life, but it is sure, faithful, constant and trustworthy. Clearly its activity is not that of individual beings. It is called non-action, that is to say, an activity that is real enough but invisible in the sense of non-interference. It is because of the Way that we find the wonderful emergence of the visible in the world of phenomena, and of the intelligible in the world of being. It both causes and enables things to emerge. At the level of the Way there is no difference between doing and letting be, but it is necessary to the Way that one must go back in order to discover the Great Ancestor from whom proceeds all that is. *Nemo tam Pater,* 'Our Mother', who is beyond Heaven-and-Earth. As everything proceeds from it, human discourse can allude to it, without being able to define it, let alone explain it, impose a structure on it or search out its meaning. In the eyes of the Chinese, structuralism is folly if one tries to substitute it for the Way, but it is a good formula if one looks to it for a trustworthy manifestation of beings which are produced or else produce themselves. Being produced always *looks* the same as producing oneself. But whatever happens there must be the antecedence, the ancestral priority of the Way. Through its Virtue (which is like its handmaid) the Way makes Heaven-and-Earth follow a motion which, because it is self-regulating, allows for a slight oscillation round the constant (the Way). If something is missing, or if some being loses its direction, the Way has nothing to do with it. It turns unceasingly, but without suffering corruption (Lao Tzu *The Book of the Way and of Virtue*, ch. 25). Supremely great, the Way is a Sovereign, and a master too, because it teaches simply by being what it is. 'I am so manifestly present in my creation', Péguy used to say, after the Psalm, *Coeli ennarrant*. . . . Just as the Empire cannot exist without the Emperor, so Heaven-and-Earth and all they contain cannot exist without the Way. The Emperor who imitates the Way, through his obedience to Heaven and his gesture of attentive submission to the Earth, exercises throughout the Empire an authoritative influence which reaches through, in each individual being, to the form of activity that is proper to it. Take from the Sovereign the imperial headdress and the robe embroidered with nine dragons; take from him his attendants and advisers, his throne and his throne room, his palace and even his accumulated wealth, and he will still remain the sovereign. Everything that stirs in the Empire only does so through him. His immobility, silence and invisibility, far from diminishing his power, make it more spiritual, more efficacious, more majestic. He resembles in that moment the polar star which, motionless, silent and scarcely visible, disposes around itself the apparent movement of the heavens.

The question will be asked: does the Way produce or does it engender? What connection does it maintain with what is produced or engendered? No reply can be given to these questions as long as they remain at the level of words. But one can grasp the thinking that lies behind them, and this is analogous to that perceived in the Book of Genesis: Elohim said, 'Let there be light, and there was light' (Dhorme), or else: Elohim said, 'The light will be, and the light is' (Chouraqui). In either case the connection between Elohim and the production of light is immediate, effortless, natural. It is the action of God through non-action, through non-interference. In Genesis Elohim *speaks* and his word is efficacious. In a Chinese version of the Creation the Way does not speak; it *is* and its being is efficacious. The anthropomorphism of Genesis is more obvious, but the author knows quite well that it is in *being* that God, Elohim creates, or, if one prefers it, the word of Elohim is wholly spiritual. From the point of view of transcendence, both Elohim and the Way are with all beings, engendered or produced, in a relationship of ascendence which places them above all created things: they are really transcendent.

I have no space to develop here a point which is not unrelated to this question of the Transcendence of the Way. The point I refer to is the following: with the Way exists its Virtue, and I do not think it would be imprudent to regard them as a couple—Reality in itself and its efficacious manifestation—so that, in spite of its absolute transcendence, within itself but not in contra-distinction to itself, the Way would possess Virtue. They are Two which exist as One. Virtue proceeds from the Way, the Way does not proceed from Virtue. The relationship between the Way and Virtue is expressed most clearly in chapter 38 of Lao Tzu. Returning to the text on which we began to comment (Chuang Tzu, chapter 6) we note that the Way exists at one and the same time above all beings and in the inmost depths of all that proceeds from it. It is never what it makes, and all that exists proceeds from it. What better transcendence could one find than absolute immanence, what better immanence than absolute transcendence? Is not the engineer who invents Concorde or designs the Tancarville Bridge immanent to these constructions, while at the same time transcending all constructions? Our text says so categorically: the Way creates spirits but is not itself a spirit; it creates both Heaven and Earth, but is neither high like Heaven nor abyssal like the unfathomed womb of the Earth. Earth and Heaven have a continuous existence, but the Way exists outside duration. It propagates, communicates and transmits itself, but those that it influences do not possess it or make it their own.

It should be clear from what has just been said that Transcendence, for the Taoists, expresses a (divine) presence beyond man, and even beyond Heaven itself, and that immanence likewise is for them a (divine) presence which is closer to man than his own heart, closer than the profound earthly depths where the essential beings and their will to exist have their origin. All this is elementary, and an inadequate basis on which to argue for the originality of Chinese thought. Following the logical movement natural to the Chinese, and entering *in medias res*, one still needs to ask oneself where and how the *admirabile commercium*, the wonderful exchange between Transcendence and Immanence takes place—where, except in the median void? how, except through non-action? What makes a thought Chinese is the fact that it expresses a complex web of contradictions, the moment when the rival tendencies meet, and the reunion which ensures that those seeking to unite with one another meet and find life. There is always an area of apparent emptiness and ceaseless activity. According to the Chinese mind, Transcendence and Immanence, which are simply the two contrasting aspects of Reality which surpasses us, are the action of non-interference, the action of non-action, the *Wei Wu Wei*. As Lao Tzu has said, speaking, in chapter 3, of the Sacred Kings of antiquity, who are the human image of what is most perfect in the Way:

The Holy Ones . . .
Acted through non-action
And nothing was wanting in their conduct.

Whichever being made Heaven and the Earth is so close to this Heaven-and-Earth that it expresses itself through the natural activity of all beings, which in turn reveals his non-active presence. The (divine) non-action makes possible the freedom of man, and the spontaneity of all other living beings and of the inanimate world itself (which is only inanimate for us occidentals). The silence, the overwhelming sensible absence of God makes possible the Song of the Universe and the teeming variety of all that has form and colour.

As I reach the end of these reflections, I come back to what is inadequate about the religion of the Chinese. While it is true that the individuals who come onto the stage of written tradition do not lack 'presence', they do not possess what we would call a personal consciousness. The personalism of Mounier is alien to the Chinese. Painfully aware of the mystery of ephemeral existence, they submit to birth and death more as to movements of nature than as to events in a process of personal growth. Yet in the conduct of their lives they manifest real integrity and moral strength. In becoming disciples of a 'Way', they are seeking to do with Heaven wants them to do—Heaven, Way of Heaven, Great Ancestor, Our Master, source of inward torment, present and always out of reach! Suspicious of the anthropomorphic notion of God which was prevalent in former times, they prefer to commit themselves to 'That' which is greater than any human person. They are 'probablists', not in the moral but in the metaphysical sense. They lack assurance in the face of God, being uncertain about 'That' which he is and therefore of 'That' which they are themselves. How should we criticise them? Is it a crime, when one is in a state of agonising uncertainty, to 'act as if'? Especially when the 'as if' refers neither to God's existence nor to one's own, but to one's impossibility of knowing 'who' is 'what'. If we Christians did not know, through faith, that the transcendent God has come close to us in Jesus Christ, and makes us sons in the Son, what kind of certainty would we have? Is not the fear of death, which is sometimes enough to wake us up in the middle of the night, a reminder that the coherence of our being does not come from within ourselves?

Translated by Sarah Fawcett

Notes

1. In 1939 Pius XI declared that Chinese rites are not superstitious in themselves. Christians may practise them.

2. *Humanisme chinois, spiritualité chrétienne* (Casterman 1964), preface p. 8.

3. The most celebrated in his autobiography *Beyond East and West* (London 1952).

4. *The Book of the Way and of Virtue*: See, for instance, the translation by Arthur Wally (London 1934).

Jean Charbonnier

The Reinterpretation of Western Christianity in terms of China Past and Present

THE very idea of 'Western Christianity' derives from China. Chinese intellectuals, whether educated people of the past or present-day revolutionaries, use the term to cover all the phenomena of Christianity. They apply it to the religion of the Europeans who came from the 'great West', irrespective of whether they were Catholics or Protestants, and belonged to the Latin or the Eastern Church. In Chinese eyes, the world-wide distribution of Christianity in no way diminishes its essentially western character. In America, Africa or Asia, Christianity bears the marks of its European origins. Unlike Buddhism, which came from the West in the early centuries of our era, Christianity is not recognised as a Chinese religion. As for the presence of Christians in third-world countries such as Latin America, the Philippines and Black Africa, the Chinese appear to see that as no more than the result of European colonial incursions since the sixteenth century.

This use of 'Western' is a disadvantage for Christianity which conceives itself as a universal salvific religion. It imposes bounds on Christianity which are really no more than geographical. 'Western' means a civilisation different from Chinese civilisation. Christianity is seen as an integral part of that Western civilisation. Since the sixteenth century missionaries have tried to show that this religion is superior to the wisdom of China. But the aggressive and greedy behaviour of Europeans seemed to prove the opposite. The Chinese revolution of our own times has rejected Christianity because it is essentially a ratification of Western imperialism.

It is useless to argue that modern Europe is de-Christianised and that Christianity should not be confused with the economic and political domination of the West. Whether they were sincere or not, the nineteenth-century colonisers were often sanctioned by Christian civilisation. Even though we no longer refer to the 'Christian West', it is still possible to speak of Western Christianity. And in fact Christians are still more numerous in the rich countries of the Western world.

The Westerners spread in China the ideals of justice, peace and charity. At the same time they humiliated a secular culture and through their commercial practice helped to exploit a people forced to undergo a great suffering and misery. The modern Chinese have taken up these ideals and cite them against Western pretensions. Surely, then, Christianity is a false ideology? Western Christians are required to justify themselves. In order to give an authentic account of their faith, they have to reinterpret the meaning of their presence in society. To do that they must be fully aware of the nature of the challenge from China.

THE WISDOM OF CHINA AND CHRISTIAN HUMANISM

For some four centuries Chinese resistance to Christian teaching has represented a dual challenge: on the one hand, a rejection of a religion judged to be injurious to the interests of China; and on the other hand, complete confidence in a Chinese wisdom that ensures the political order and the well-being of the people.

The successes of Matteo Ricci among some nonconformist members of the educated classes represented in the Reformist Party of Tunglin[1] should not make us forget the attacks which Ricci had to suffer from conservative intellectuals.[2] They criticised the main lines of his *T'ien chu shih yi* (*The True Meaning of God*), an introduction to Christian doctrine which, however, pays the greatest possible attention to the traditions of Chinese wisdom.[3] To be sure the best-intentioned of these critics had to agree that most of these teachings was acceptable since they were already to be found in Chinese tradition. But they saw Ricci as discredited by defending insupportable ideas about God, creation and the after-life. Though they appreciated his scientific and moral contribution, they cavilled at his religious inadequacies. Their essential plaint was directed against even the cult of the Lord of heaven (*T'ien chu*, translating the word 'God'). This form of worship seemed to them irreconcilable with the ritual hierarchy of the Empire and the Confucian rules of filial piety (*hsiao*). Ricci suggests that all men are equal before the Lord of heaven and that everyone can address in prayer without the mediation of the

Emperor. Yet the Emperor is traditionally the only person competent to offer a sacrifice to heaven. Worse, the Western intellectual (*hsi ju*) dares to state that we must worship the Lord of heaven above everything and everybody else, even before his father and mother, and even before the monarch. Three sacred principles of *hsiao* are involved here: submission of a subject to the sovereign, of a son to his father, and of a woman to her husband.

Some intellectuals attacked not only Christian teaching but Church organisation. Yang Kuang-hsien, not without an interest in obtaining court patronage, showed that Christians were subversive elements who were trying to overthrow the imperial order; they held assemblies (so he charged) and established mixed communities of men and women as in heterodox Chinese sects. These communities communicated with one another; they comprised a spy network throughout the Empire; and they were in touch with foreign powers via Macao. Finally Christians owed allegiance to an Emperor in religion (*chiao-huang* = pope) who lived in Rome.

The intellectuals condemned *inter alia* the activities of the Sicilian Jesuit Longobardi in the south of China and accused the missionaries of destroying statues on altars and of teaching country-folk to rebel against the sacred ones. Even before the Roman condemnation of the ancestral rites, Christians were already thought of as bad citizens.

These accusations, often most emphatically couched, were not without foundation. Though seventeenth-century Christian Europe was not in a position to conquer China as Spain had done a large part of South America, the Catholic missions nevertheless dreamed of a peaceful conversion of the entire country. Matteo Ricci paid his own way to Peking in order to contact the Emperor himself. He succeeded in offering him a painting of the Saviour and was granted a short-lived hope of the realisation of his dearest dream: the conversion of the Emperor who, as a later-day Constantine, would call all his immense Empire to the banner of Christ.[4] We should not be astonished at these ambitions which live on in the minds of some present-day missiologists. Many of the regrets expressed over the disappearance of the Chinese rites rely on the implicit idea that all China would probably have been converted if they had not been forbidden.

The Jesuits of the seventeenth and eighteenth centuries were unstinting in their admiration of Chinese civilisation. Like the accounts of Marco Polo in the thirteenth century, their *Edifying Letters*[5] helped to spread throughout Europe the image of an orderly China replete with moral virtues. Educated according to the notions of an essentially classical humanism, they were able to offer in China a Christianity favourable to reason and morality. They had to do so in order to obtain any audience at all. The riches of China were expended *ad maiorem Dei gloriam*. urely it was possible for a Europe weakened by religious wars and fratricidal struggles between monarchs to win inspiration from the order and reason that reigned in the Chinese Empire?

The challenge from China did not leave European intellectuals untouched. China became a contradictory symbol for two major conflicting tendencies in theology. Jansenist-influenced circles, the *devôts* and associated groups, who for some time had been uneasy over the humanistic trends represented by the Jesuits, did not believe in this supposedly virtuous China which might well remove the very essence of salvation—the wretchedness of fallen man and the operation of grace. In his fifth *lettre Provinciale* Pascal accused the Jesuits of eliminating the scandal of the cross in China. The allies of the Jesuits were on the contrary intellectuals and philosophers searching for rational bases for morals and politics. Towards the end of the seventeenth century Leibniz expressed his approval of the despatch of the Jesuit mathematicians to China. He saw them as instruments of the religious unity of the world; while showing forth the true theology, they allowed Westerners to learn from the Chinese 'the art of governing and that entire natural theology which they have taken to so high a point of perfection'.[6] Voltaire sided with Leibniz against Bayle in approving the deism of the Chinese, but from their natural morality he drew extreme conclusions in regard to the authority of the Church and the Bible. China, he declared, had been able to organise itself with tolerance and without the aid of superstition. The materialist philosophers had only a little way to go in order to show that the Chinese were in fact atheists and that paradise there was of course Nature. The Communist historian Chu Ch'ien-chih found no difficulty in stating that the introduction of Chinese thought to Europe in the eighteenth century contributed to the birth of Western dialectical materialism.[7]

THE CHALLENGE OF MAOISM TO THE MODERN THEOLOGY OF THE WORLD

Perhaps the challenge of the new China to our present-day Western society is no more than the logical conclusion of the premises established three centuries ago. Today, too, the essence of the debate has to do with a philosophy of man and of society.

Now, however, Christianity is more radically called in question. The Enlightenment philosophy was directed mainly against the oppressive power of an ecclesiastical institution inimical to science and progress, and against the privileges of an obscurantist clergy. Nowadays it is the theologians themselves and leading churchmen who are concerned with the challenge of China, and Chinese atheism confronts contemporary versions of Christian thought.

Since 1974 a theological research movement set up by ecumenical conferences at Båstad, Sweden (January 29-February 2, 1974), and Louvain (September 9-14, 1974) has been trying to discover the theological implications of the new China.[8] The attention given to 'Maoism' probably betrays a tendency to conceptualisation peculiar to Western European thinking. Much more than the problems of a Chinese society undergoing modernisation, it is the thought of Mao Tse-tung which seems to have intrigued Christian intellectuals. They have found the Cultural Revolution of 1966 much more interesting than the entry of China to the United Nations in 1971.

The present investigations undertaken by Western theologians accord with a long process of development in Western European thought. Whereas in the eighteenth century the current deism had hardly any time for theology, the great thinkers of the nineteenth century brought religion down from heaven to earth. With Feuerbach theology was inverted to become anthropology. Karl Marx drew the appropriate conclusions in political economy. For him religion was only the dream of a suffering mankind alienated by conditions of production that made them no more than slaves. Consequently the fulfilment of man should bring about the disappearance of all religion sooner or later. Suspected of being sowers of lies and of denying men the right to live and to be free, theologians were forced to take earthly reality seriously. The result has been a reinterpretation of Christian life.

Whereas formerly they were asked to reject the temptations of the world, Christians are now encouraged to love this world and to transform it through justice and love. Hence the rise of theologies of the laity, work, development, liberation, hominisation and secularisation. Theologians tend nowadays to emphasise the doctrines of the Incarnation and creation. The present world, they stress, is the very location of salvation: 'God so loved the world that he gave to it his only Son'. Christ's death on the cross was not humiliating but the foundation of human autonomy. The Christian faith is not alienating but liberating. It is committed to a transformation of the world as testimony to a continuous progress towards the Kingdom of heaven.

Carried along by this tendency to exalt mankind, some people probably go so far as to believe that the Chinese experiment is grist to their mill. But the Chinese, for their part, hardly seem impressed. Is this vocabulary of liberation really sincere? We must remember what Mao Tse-tung said to the journalist Anna Louise Strong. When he asked her what was the core of the Christian message, she replied: 'To free the captives'. Mao

Tse-tung in his turn replied curtly: 'And what exactly have you done to achieve that?'

That is no mere accusation of practical impotence. Less naïvely than that, Mao believed that the development of Chinese society depended on the energies of the Chinese people alone and required no appeal to any supernatural power. Mao proclaimed in the name of popular creativity the very human autonomy that Western theologians assert in the name of the love of God. Far from ignoring the spiritual dimensions of man, this creative dynamism of the people is inspired by elevated ethical ideals. The Maoist ideal of the New Man appears to surmount the defects of the Western society of productivity and consumption. Chinese development is accompanied by an immense effort towards human education aiming at a reduction of inequality and a gradual elimination of all exploitation of man by man.

The most revolutionary theological statements are challenged by this. Religious talk about liberation seems superfluous or at the very least relative. It is surely significant that theologians of liberation, while taking inspiration from Maoist methodology and perspectives, hardly engage with the trend of theological thought actually provoked by China.

European and American theologians on the other hand play a prominent part in this search. Committed to the trend to Western secularisation, they see China as an immense echo-chamber of their criticisms of the outworn inheritance of Christianity. The Chinese Revolution, which is both atheist and deeply human, prizes the vision of a human liberation established on the basis of the idea of the death of God. The Chinese rejection of religious rites and any institutional Church seems appropriately to dissolve the bonds which the Christian authorities insist on maintaining with the power or riches of this world. But what we must go on to show is that this secular revolution can have a Christian significance.

SECULARISATION OF CHRISTIAN SALVATION AND SACRALISATION OF THE CHINESE REVOLUTION

An internal contradiction undermines theological thought about China. China is so useful an aid in the secularisation of Christianity that it could end in abolishing it. Sensing this danger, some people react by sacralising the Chinese experiment.

According to Raymond Whitehead,[9] the Chinese Revolution announces what could be a Christianity that is both radical and secular. The Chinese Revolution is an authentic salvation outside the Church. It revitalises Christian salvation. Though certainly incomplete, for it demands a permanent revolution, it is in this respect comparable to the continuous progress of Christians towards the Kingdom. An exchange therefore seems desirable between these two conceptions of salvation. The Maoist notion of class struggle in particular may serve to clarify our idea of Christian love. Our assertion of universal love is often too abstract. An authentic love is always historically committed and cannot make an abstraction of class differences. The contrary of love is not hatred but apathy and omission.

On an ethical level, love may easily be interpreted in a secular mode. But what about grace and the cross in this regard? Whitehead suggests that the Maoist faith in an inevitable liberation may be seen as a form of grace inasmuch as it envisions a force of Justice at the heart of the universe. As for the cross, it is not a sign of impotence but an act of identification with the oppressed, the death of a slave by means of which the humble are to be elevated. Whitehead declares that the cross is a sign of hope and struggle, resurrection and revolt.

The possibility of a secular intepretation of Christianity in Maoist terms would seem to be supported by the foregoing. But in what does the exchange between these two forms of mysticism consist? So far one of two supposedly interchangeable realities replaces another. Perhaps they are interchangeable at this secular level of ideologico-political struggle. But it is difficult now to decide exactly what their mutual contributions might be. The Maoist idea of love enriches Christian love while criticising its liberal deviations. But does Christian love offer anything to the Chinese? There is nothing here of the very core of Christian love—love incarnated in the person of Christ and the people of God, a love whose ultimate aim is a divinisation of man by means of adoption into sonhood. This religious language expresses an original experience which has to be taken into account.

But instead of stating exactly what is specific to the Christian message, some thinkers avoid the loss of meaning in their faith by sacralising the Chinese experiment. They take care in the process not to subject it (like Christianity) to the test of secularisation. Basing themselves on the phenomenology of religion, they find in Maoist China all the external signs of a religion. A book by Ninian Smart takes this stance very firmly.[10] In this perspective, Maoism has its dogmas, celebrations, personality cult, myth of last ends, call to conversion, confessions, and promise of a new life. The Chinese Revolution has its heroes and its martyrs. The Little Red Book is a catechism. The red sun of Mao Tse-tung resembles the universal illumination of the Buddha. This religion is not belief in God but faith in the people, and the well-being of the people may demand human sacrifice. It is an eschatological struggle between Light and the

Darkness. Good is the liberation of the people, whereas evil is imperialism and feudalism.

Is Maoism, then, a new religion? To assert that would be to make a value-judgment in a sense not permitted by the sociology of religion. We must remember that Mao Tse-tung himself always declared that he was anti-religious. He never conceived of a kind of positivist religion in the manner of Comte. He always desired the destruction of the temples. He tolerated the cult of his personality only during the Cultural Revolution. Today the Little Red Book is hardly seen in China, and references to the great liberator are rare. Chinese celebrations, even for the New Year, remain strictly civic and family occasions. The First of May and the National Day on October 1 are no more religious than the 'sacred love of the fatherland' hymned by French Republicans of unimpeachable secularism.

The sacred, some would say, is not the essence of the religious, but the transcendent is.[11] But what do we mean by 'the transcendent'? Is it the supernatural? Maoism excludes that, both in terms of Marxist atheism and of Chinese humanist tradition. The distinction between nature and supernature has been used in the West to express the otherness of God and the gift of his salvific love. But for the Chinese the idea of the supernatural evokes the threat of occult powers and of fate. Confucius said that that was something to beware of. If there is any transcendence in China, it is to be found in the notion of a fulfilment of mankind wholly in control of its destiny. In fact the Chinese ways to transcendence remain to be explored. The external manifestations of the sacred are insufficient to allow us to assess those dimensions adequately. To insert everything in the category of the sacred is as sterile an operation as a contrary levelling-down into the category of the secular.

THE CONFLICT OF TWO UNIVERSALISMS

The tendency of Western secularisation is paradoxically accompanied by a trend towards the sacralisation of the Chinese experience. What are the reasons for this process? Are we to see it as a kind of compensation for the loss of meaning from which our society is suffering? The interest in Maoist mysticism is perhaps no more than a manifestation of the Western taste for Eastern forms of spirituality.

We may also be in the presence of an inverse self-defensive reaction on the part of Christians. To describe Maoism as a new religion is to suggest that it is a false religion, a form of idolatry, a 'Maolatry'. At best one may acknowledge the merits of Chinese revolutionary mysticism, but in order to see in them the traces of Christian salvation extended to China in a form more or less distorted by Marxism.

Catholic theology of religion tends traditionally to gather the values of different civilisations under the all-encompassing cloak of the Church. Hence it arrogates to itself the right to deprive them of their specific values. The Greek Fathers cited the case of the Jewish people carrying off in their Exodus the jewels of the Egyptians. That would seem to have been the attitude of the Fides Agency in 1973 when its editor discerned in China tendencies that reflected pontifical and conciliar teachings: 'Present-day China tends towards a mysticism of disinterested work in the service of others, towards an aspiration to justice, an exaltation of the simple and frugal way of life, an elevation of the peasant masses and a mixture of social classes. But surely it is here precisely that we find what has been said and re-said in an incomparable way in the encyclicals *Pacem in terris* and *Populorum progressio*, and in the synodal document *Justice in the World*? Today the Chinese masses are being taught to form a communitarian consciousness. But surely that is what the Second Vatican Council so emphatically required of the people of God?'[12]

It is certainly unfortunate that the 'Chinese masses' are not perceptive enough to see that they are Christians without knowing it. In any case they are not at all prepared to allow Westerners to lay claim to what they themselves won by armed struggle in the name of national independence. It was in fact the Chinese who took from the West what might assist the progress of their people. They have culled from Western Christianity values which remained sterile in order to make them bear fruit in a new people. Within the perspective of their own Chinese universalism they have appropriated certain values of Western Christianity, just as Christian universalism would like to appropriate the values of the Chinese Revolution. The Chinese Revolution inherits a cultural messianism just as powerful as that of the Christians. This messianism is just as much established on the history of a people, and that history develops by virtue of a revolutionary dialectic of the rebellion of exploited peasants against the powers of oppression. The sole justification of power is to be found in an alliance of Wisdom (*Tao*) and Government (*chih*). The nation is on the way towards a Great Unity (*Ta t'ung*) in which the Chinese of today can recognise the classless society of Marxism. That will be the advent of a New Man, freed from all mutual exploitation. All the nations of the world will then be summoned to the universal brotherhood of 'one family under heaven'.

This Sinocentric view of the future of mankind forms a whole comparable to the Europeocentric conception descended from the Judaeo-Christian tradition of salvation. To the extent that the de-Christianised West is losing touch with its redemptive horizon, it can be tempting to think of a universal transference of the Christian mission of salvation to a new nation coming to fruition in the Chinese world. The Formosan Presbyterian theologian Song Choan-seng is not afraid to locate a new phase in the history of salvation in China.[13] Three thousand years passed after the period opened up by the Exodus of Israel. Mao Tse-tung's Long March initiated, so Choan-seng claims, a new phase of human history. There is of course no dichotomy between the history of salvation and the history of the world. God acts in world history. Therefore it is not necessary, he concludes, to proceed though the mediation of biblical history, but only to discern in various cultural contexts the events that are characteristic of God's creative and redemptive action. This salvific action is defined as a breaking down of the barriers of enslavement and an opening up both to God and to man. Initially the Chinese Revolution was a movement of liberation from poverty, hunger and exploitation. Confronted with the new forms of exploitation which have appeared in the present régime, it should become a struggle for freedom of spirit. It was such a struggle when the people of Israel made the transition from nomadism to national structures. The indomitable spirit of the prophets alone was able to put up a fight against ideological sclerosis.

This transference of mission proposed by Song Choan-seng is not unambiguous. Biblical reference to the creative and redemptive God remains indispensable. As for the dual liberation from economic and spiritual slavery, there is no ground for asserting that China has a monopoly in that regard. That would be merely to substitute a Christian-Chinese cultural universalism for the Christian-Western cultural universalism. No specific civilisation can claim a monopoly over the salvation of mankind.

Must we then resign ourselves to a mere pluralism of modes of human liberation? But how then are we to do justice to the universal perspective characteristic of these messages of salvation?

TOWARDS A CRITICAL CATEGORISATION OF SPECIFIC MODES OF SALVATION

Western thought remains abstract and tends to universalise in spite of the onslaught of Marxist critiques. A more extended sociological and historical analysis of the two Christian-Western and Marxist-Chinese structures should help us to overcome the contradictions noted between the religious and the secular aspects or the the two universalisms. Some useful distinctions have already been made within the framework of European ecumenical research, in particular in the form of the binary oppositions of myth and reality, and faith and ideology.

Whereas ideologists are fascinated by the Maoist myth of the New Man, practitioners, whether Sinologists or former missionaries, pay more attention to the actual conditions of life in China.[14] Chinese theologians from Hong Kong for their part condemn new forms of oppression which have developed in the course of the Cultural Revolution. This criticism on the basis of the facts follows the logical trend of Marxism itself, which declares that any idealisation without reference to practice is false ideology. When it accords with an actual phase of human development, the myth of the New Man acts as a fruitful utopia. If it merely serves to cover economic setbacks, social disorder or conflicts between political factions, the same myth becomes mystification, an idealist falsification of history. It is necessary to take the same critical distance with regard to Christian ideals. China justly reminds Christians of the degree to which their words can be distant from their actions.

Ideology, in the sense of a systematic expression of a vision of human life, can play a positive or a negative role.[15] If it arises from an improved understanding of human reality in progress, it is progressive. If on the contrary it hardens into a dogma imposed on society by a totalitarian power, it is a conservative force. There is a Christian ideology inspired by faith in Christ. It combines an ideological expression of belief with socio-political elements. This ideology can become dogmatic and oppressive if it acts as a sanction for domination by privileged individuals or classes. Only a living faith in Love incarnate among the poorest of all is able to renew it. There is also a Marxist ideology which arose from the proletarian revolution and from faith in the liberation of the people. This ideology is intended to be progressive while remaining linked with the actual practice of the masses. It is no less susceptible for that reason of development into a rigid and formalistic dogmatism which serves to legitimise the totalitarian power of the Communist Party. Only actual openness to the voice of the people can renew it. Christian faith in the incarnate Word and Marxist faith in the people are different in nature, as has to be demonstrated, but the two are living experiences able to inspire a criticism of ideologies which have descended to the level of instruments of oppression of human freedom.

If we submit both of them to the scrutiny of Marxist criticism, the Christian and Chinese ways are in fact far from mutually exclusive. They even tend to a mutual approximation. The Christian way is following a more earthly route after having been blocked for a long time by the Platonising dissociation of soul and body. The Chinese way, which was for a long time imprisoned by a fatalism of historical cycles, is now opening up towards the horizon of a new people working for justice and peace in the world.

If the Chinese experiment is taken into consideration it helps us to

restrict the ambitions of a non-critical Christianity produced by a domina-
tive Christianity with Europe as its centre. The elimination of Christianity
by China is not, however, any more justifiable than a Christian monopoly
of salvation. The new China has criticised its conservative Confucian
tradition just as Europe has criticised its Christian institutions. When
dissociated in principle from power, the Christian and Chinese forms of
wisdom are perhaps rejected in terms of a purely private inward experience. It is an urgent task to see more clearly the originality of the
Christian, Buddhist, Taoist and Confucian forms of experience, and to
decide how they might enrich and renew the life of the people. We would
wish that the scientific effort of China in the human sciences might
contribute to a phase of international co-operation in comparative religion. There is room for fruitful communication between the Peking Institute for the Study of World Religions and various Christian centres for
the study of religion in Hong Kong, Kyoto, Manila and Singapore, as well
as in India, Europe and America.

Freed from their feeling of superiority, Christians could enter con-
fidently on this task. Their own religious tradition, if more exactly defined
and more appropriately located in the life of the world, remains an
essential element of human history. The mutual confrontation of East
and West should be replaced by a fertile era of inter-cultural exchange.

Translated by J. G. Cumming

Notes

1. The Tunglin Academy was founded in the twelfth century at Wuhsi and restored in 1604; it brought together intellectuals critical of abuses of power in the name of Neo-Confucian orthodoxy.

2. The most noteworthy collections of anti-Christian writings of the seventeenth century are the *P'o hsieh chi*, which appeared in Fuchien province in 1639, and the *P'i hsieh lun* of Yang Kuang-hsien (1659); these two titles mean 'refutation of heresy'.

3. The *T'ien chu shih yi* is not a catechism but a 'justification of God' in terms of Chinese beliefs. This treatise was written in 1596 and printed in 1604. An old translation appeared in *Lettres édifiantes et curieuses* (Paris) vol. iv pp. 380-453.

4. See Henri Bernard SJ *Le père Matthieu Ricci et la société chinoise de son temps* (1552-1610) (Tientsin 1937) vol. 2 pp. 5-19.

5. Abridged for *Lettres édifiantes et curieuses écrites des missions étrangères par quelques missionnaires de la Compagnie de Jésus*, 34 vols (1702-1776).

6. Extracted from a preface by Leibniz to a book on the Edict of Tolerance of 1697 authorising Christian worship in China, quoted by Virgile Pinot in *La Chine et la formation de l'esprit philosophique en France* (1640-1740) (Paris 1932) pp. 335-6.

7. Chu Ch'ien-chih 'Questions sur l'objet et le domaine de l'histoire de la philosophie chinoise', in *Chungkuo chêhsueh shih went'i t'aolun chuanchi*, a collection of discussions of the history of Chinese philosophy (Peking 1957) p. 90.

8. The documents from Båstad and Louvain were published as *Christianity and the New China* (Pasadena 1976). A first, duplicated edition was circulated in 1974 by Pro Mundi Vita and the International Lutheran Church Federation: Vol. I (Båstad) *Theological Implications of the New China*; vol. 2 (Louvain) *Christian Faith and the Chinese Experience*.

9. Raymond Whitehead 'Love and Animosity in the Ethic of Mao', in the Båstad documents (vol. I) pp. 71-85.

10. Ninian Smart *Mao* (London 1974).

11. See Paul Rule 'Is Maoism open to the Transcendent' in *The New China: A Catholic Response* ed. Michael Chu SJ (New York 1977) pp. 25-43.

12. International Fides Agency (Rome, April 4, 1973).

13. Song Choan-seng, 'The New China and Salvation History: A Methodological Inquiry', in the Båstad documents (vol. I) pp. 113-33.

14. '"New Man" in China: Myth or Reality?' in the Louvain documents (vol. II) pp. 45-58.

15. On this point see Winifried Gluër 'Faith and Ideology in the Context of the New China', Båstad Documents pp. 37-53; Julia Ching 'Faith and Ideology in the Light of the New China' Båstad Documents, first edition pp. 15-36.

Luigi Sartori

The Theological Theme of
Salvation and Liberation
and the Maoist Concept
of a New Humanity

OUR theology still lacks a systematic treatment of the theme of 'salvation'.[1] During the course of history Christian thought has produced
'fragments'; the full picture has not yet been completed. The following
five steps contributed important 'fragments': the acceptance of the Old
Testament into the Biblical canon, even though the emphasis was on
typological interpretation, helped to broaden and particularise the idea of
'liberation'; St Augustine's insistence on freedom as 'grace', on man's
radical insufficiency, the need for surrender and prayer so that freedom
does not remain a pure abstraction; the value given to human endeavour
in the famous disputes on the relationship between freedom and grace,
against laxist and fatalistic tendencies; the emphasis in modern times in
social and political ethics on the way in which structures and institutions
condition people and thus determine their relative freedom or slavery;
the current recognition of the co-operation of certain 'specific' factors in
human salvation, both in the 'temporal' sphere and in the 'spiritual', so
that the Church is not the only force for salvation and has no monopoly in
it.

But why only 'fragments'? Although this is an over-simplification
perhaps the explanation is this: up till now the process of 'liberation' has
been considered as an historical fact accomplished once and for all in
history. The 'history of salvation' is merely recalled or celebrated in the
liturgy. Between here and eternity there is a kind of 'millennarianism', the

dream of enjoying henceforth the rewards for our labours in the exhaust-
ing and now completed march towards freedom.[2]

Today, however, Christianity has providentially been sent back to
square one. It must begin all over again. In the West it has been battered
by secularisation. Latin America, Africa and Asia are feeling the awaken-
ing of new hopes for new ways to freedom. Perhaps the Chinese situation
is the one nearest to the biblical. In Latin America, for example, the old
and the new are still too intermingled and the enemies of freedom often
call themselves Christians. Africa is a melting pot of many different
struggles. Only China is a united people trying to move towards the
freedom of a new humanity. In the case of China we are still faced with the
radical theological problem of hermeneutics which arose with the biblical
canon. Is only an allegorical and typological interpretation permissible?
Or can we speak of real stages in an authentic history of salvation, a
pilgrimage (or what could be a pilgrimage) towards Christ?[3]

This article tries to answer the question. But we are taking a long view,
which almost amounts to no more than a methodology. We look at the
theme of Christian liberation under three headings: the point of depar-
ture, the point of arrival, and the seekers themselves.

1. THE STARTING POINT: REAL PEOPLE, ESPECIALLY THE POOR AND OPPRESSED

Christian wisdom begins with a story which must be lived through
before it can be understood. Jesus 'began to do and to teach' (Acts 1:1).
Only later did theology reverse this, preferring a deductive method
offering an ideology from which practical applications could be drawn.
Marxism stimulates Christianity to recover the primacy of action, not of
course blind, fideistic irrational action, but action which is aware and
meaningful for the fate of humanity and the universe. For Christianity the
beginning is the life of a prophet, Jesus.

In particular Christians could benefit from the Maoist demand for a
constant and fruitful relationship between theory and practice, to act as a
permanent check and counter-check against the temptation to capricious
subjectivism or stubborn dogmatism.[4] Every step must be checked
because any 'wisdom' can act as a cover for falsehoods and become an
ideology.[5] Maoism lays stress on caution towards dogmatism. It is not
content with a revolution of 'structures' but also strives for a parallel
revolution of 'culture'; it insists on 'education' because ideas are the
moving force of history.[6]

Christian wisdom is bound up with the incarnation; it cannot speak of a new human being in the abstract. Human salvation requires the *discernment of real needs*, and the actual situations people are in when they start out on the road to freedom. Wisdom is not afraid of science, but calls it to aid. Appealing to values alone is not enough. The evils from which people need to be freed must be 'named'. Classical theology using Pauline language speaks of Christ freeing us from 'death', 'sin' and the 'devil' (see Rom. 5-6), to describe mankind's total wretchedness. We need the constant help of science to identify the real and particular aspects of this evil which enslaves us. Just as God is hidden behind all positive values, so is Satan behind all particular evils. Theology and pastoral care must emerge from their habit of generalising and abstraction, and name particular goals to be striven for in the process of human liberation.

The danger of ideology cannot be overcome once and for all. Mao seemed to be aware of this and the only thing he exempted from permanent criticism was the fundamental choice of striving for the good of all the people and the abolition of a dominant oppressive class.[7] I think that Christian salvation must also be based on *one single permanent choice: to side with the poor, the 'last'*. Because this was the choice Christ made; in him God 'became poor' (2 Cor. 8:9). This is because the process of liberation is the more genuine, the lower its starting point. Those who are down have no privileges to defend and so they are prepared to look towards a total salvation for all. People who are already rich and established threaten to place obstacles in the way of others. Saving all mankind, saving all people risks remaining an illusion if it does not start from the lowest, if the lowest do not engage in it.

The 'updating' by Vatican II sanctioned this direction. In line with the four 'circles of dialogue' about which Paul VI spoke in his encyclical *Ecclesiam suam* (and realising the risk of 'ecclesiocentrism') Christian aims have become less abstract, not only because the aristocratic monopoly of the Church has been abandoned, but because the new criterion is 'co-operation', 'working together'. This is in accord with the gospel's teaching that 'the last shall be first'. *The last circle of dialogue, with people, with humanists, is therefore the touchstone for all the others.* If salvation were a theoretical announcement it would be possible to reach the 'last' by starting from the 'first'. But if it is an historical process requiring action, 'doing', then the Church must be ready to keep going back to the beginning and starting all over again with the 'last'. Alienated human beings, slaves to sin and death, must feel that they are the chief actors in the history of salvation, if Christ is its moving power. The true struggle for *libertas ecclesiae*, for Christian freedom is the struggle for 'human freedom', freedom for all people from the particular bondage in which they stand, just as Israel in Egypt was in a particular bondage.[8]

2. TOWARDS AN ESCHATOLOGICAL GOAL: THE NEW MAN IN CHRIST AND THE ABSOLUTE FUTURE

Marxism like all modern culture is based on an evolutionary view of nature. However it remains a victim to that secularisation of the Christian millennaristic heresy, which holds that the final end of history in a state of perfection is possible within this world. This is a dream of blind faith contradictory to the intrinsic mutability of everything that is 'finite'. In this respect *Maoism has had the courage to break* with this Marxist pseudo-eschatology: within their socialist society the dialectic of change continues and this leads to the demand for *permanent critical revision*.[9] This demand may also seem fideistic but echoes the classic oriental idea that becoming is infinite and illimitable.

Christian thinking, we must admit, has often fallen for the Greek predilection for the 'finite'. Time and this world have become the sphere of the 'perfect'. In theology *too much space has been given to the theme of 'human nature'*, as a collection of 'already given' gifts derived from an almost completed 'finalised' creation: history was thus only capable of bringing 'accidental' novelties, superficial modifications, more frequently described as disorder than a new order, as artificial manipulations. We Christians should not be too shocked by Mao's criticisms of the facile exaltation of 'human nature' and the ideals of freedom, equality, brotherhood, peace and love.[10] We should regain the habit of thinking of all these things as coming in the future, a future gift of God, which will also be the result of our own struggles, even through bitter conflicts, rather than as values which already exist and need only to be defended and maintained. Vatican II rediscovered the eschatological dimension as the ground of our hope of salvation. Present creation is only *a 'sketch'. Creation is history. The new human being and the new earth in Christ have only just begun.* The full revelation of Christ will only come at the end of history, and this is what gives history its dynamism. Of course there is room for philosophical discourse on 'human nature', on freedom as a gift constitutive of human dignity, which must be respected and encouraged. But this is not Christianity's 'proper work'. Christianity is interested in the real human being: the slave who needs to be freed in order to be able to be him/herself and have his/her own nature, freedom, peace and love. All these are eschatological goods. Christianity should propose them as springs of action, as the end of a process of waiting and working, gifts of grace and victories to be won. Creation is still groaning with labour pains . . . (see Rom. 8:22).

Of course the road to freedom which God in his freedom opens to us must have a 'route'. Creative events cannot be senseless leaps or sudden turnabouts. The road to wisdom must have a certain logic. Our striving must be based on a connection or *continuity between beginning and end*. But 'human nature' would remain an abstraction, in any utopia whatever, if it were not for the continual creative activity of God who alone can lead the world to its true and proper consummation.

The ethical-juridical view is not sufficient either, even though it has often dominated Christian thinking and has its basis in the Bible. In this case, history would be a theatre of rehearsals for the curtain raising at the end. The drama itself, the part played by each person on the stage of life, would not be important. The only thing that mattered would be the moral value (as with actors, the artistic talent) of the 'interpreters', because eternity would be something completely different—reward or punishment. There would be an absolute discontinuity between history and eternity. There *is* this aspect of eternity in Christian salvation but salvation cannot be *reduced* merely to an eternity of reward or punishment. Otherwise the incarnation would be meaningless. The incarnation is the mystery of God who is not only the judge at the end of history, but who also enters human history and becomes part of it, as a man among others on the road towards freedom and salvation, who takes upon himself the weight of actual human slaveries, so that the goal of history is not just judgment but also a human achievement. If we make the juridical aspect into an absolute we are guilty of the Manichean heresy, which dualises God in order to divide people into two categories, together with their world and their history.

The true Christian conception is to see in eschatology *the final fulfilment of history*, and in history the working of human beings towards the final transformation which God will bring about to fulfil and finalise our actions and intentions. It is only the hope of transformation and fulfilment 'beyond' corruptions and finite limitations that makes the call to 'permanent revolution' meaningful. Then the waiting becomes productive and is not merely a 'critical reservation' which keeps alive the sense of relativity to combat the idolators of human works which make segments of history. *The Christian is for action, just as he is for wisdom and prayer*. Prayer broadens the horizon of freedom beyond all limits by linking human action with God's. Thus the 'miracle' becomes in some sense daily bread; with God we can truly 'go beyond', beyond all limits, over the Red Sea, across the River of Jordan, in the power of the Passover which brings into being 'things that do not exist' (Rom. 4:17). Divine and human freedom take turns to work 'wonders'; this is the meaning of the 'mirabilia Dei' in the history of salvation.[11]

For this project *it is necessary for selfishness to be overcome*. Christianity has all too often over-asserted the defence of *a privatised concept of freedom*: freedom as private property, as the jealous possession of enclosed spaces, defining 'mine' and 'yours' as 'mine' beginning where 'yours' ends, and there is only peace when each person is isolated and protected in his own selfishness. God is thus reduced to being the guardian of fences and divisions! Maoism insists on the struggle against selfishness. It therefore insists that every individual life-plan should be made within a broader plan, for the whole people, and ultimately all mankind.[12] Christian freedom is real only within 'God's universal plan'. The individual is required to be prepared for 'kenosis', self-emptying, like Christ (see Phil. 2:5), in order to situate his own freedom and life-plan within the broader plan of God, the Church and mankind. True freedom is solidarity and love.

This is the only way in which we can speak meaningfully about *the content of salvation*. Nowadays we hear a great deal about the 'wholeness' of the content of freedom and salvation: spiritual goods and bodily goods, personal goods and social goods, temporal and eternal values. . . . Perhaps this was neglected in the past with too much stress laid on the spiritual. However the bodily and social and cosmic dimensions of salvation were implicit at least in two fundamental teachings: that on 'concupiscence' which remains in man as a mark of sin ('it comes from sin and leads to sin', Council of Trent) and places our need of salvation within the bodily and material; and that on the double 'ancestry' of men, recapitulated in two 'heads', Adam for evil, Christ for good, to show that salvation is a global process concerning the human race as a whole.

Thus we need to look towards a new humanity and a new world (new heaven and new earth where justice reigns) in order for the freedom of the individual to be realisable.[13] In this project 'both heaven and earth have a hand' (Dante). God's incarnation has shown that henceforth God's destiny lies within the destiny of mankind; and liberation is a pilgrimage towards the final fulness of God and his perfection which includes the fulfilment of the human and the cosmic.

3. THE ACTORS IN THE PROCESS OF LIBERATION: MAN AND GOD

The crux of the confrontation between Christianity and humanism today is the relationship between *God and man*. This is the most difficult problem about Christian salvation. History has strewn the field with difficulties. The debate which began with St Augustine plumbed the depths of human wretchedness, to stress the decisive importance of grace and thus of prayer. This gave rise to renunciatory, pessimistic and fatalistic views, which authentic Christian thinking has always resisted. Through vigorous disputes between the supporters of God's initiative and of human freedom, the importance to the problem of freedom of serving other people was discovered. Thus we can define two principal stages in Christian thinking on freedom: the appeal to God's grace shows us the *first principle* of true freedom, the emphasis on the duty to serve others shows us the *meaning and aim* of freedom. In the former freedom is seen as a 'gift', given by a God who already loves us, and thus as something that can never be reduced to something created by ourselves alone, private property jealously possessed. The latter shows freedom as a 'task', as a gift to be offered to others, as a principle of love which overflows in service and solidarity. Freedom as gift and task, as grace and service.

But today the problem is less academic. We see liberation and salvation projects undertaken by *humanists who are silent on the subject of freedom as grace, God's gift, love received*, even though they profess a conception of freedom as service. This is why China offers us a test case in the meeting between Christianity and humanism. In Mao's theories, even if not in Maoism itself, militant atheism does not dominate, but rather the positive theme of 'service to the people'.[14] In this Mao's thought reflects classical Chinese humanism, in which heaven is mirrored on earth, and the best way of proving 'true religion' is by moral action. Long before Mao the Chinese thought that the voice of Heaven was heard through the people.[15] Mao's silence about God could thus be merely discretion and respect, to concentrate attention on human moral behaviour, so that the divine may be revealed in man.

However, faith in the primacy of grace cannot mean distrust of human beings. Human beings become open to grace by prayer, only if they believe in *the limitless objective possibilities of freedom*, in particular, when they overcome the limits of selfishness and value the freedom of other people too, the freedom of all, which reaches out beyond itself to God's transcendent freedom. Mao does not oppose trust in the historical instruments placed in people's hands to genuine faith in God (the God of the incarnation who wants men to have the possibility of becoming 'sons of God'), but only to the idol, magical faith in a miracle which relieves human beings of their responsibilities.[16] It demands the transcending of selfishness.

In the Chinese case we can also see another aspect of the road that leads from the 'ethical' to the 'religious'. This is the persistence of a certain dualism between the individual and the group which is like a sort of 'transference' or 'sublimation'. Psychoanalysis speaks of the victory of the 'ego' over the 'id' through the sublimation of the 'super-ego'. In Maoism, at the socio-political level, transference seems to give the group, that is to say the whole 'people', permission to resort to violence in the sense of egoistic possession and power, because the individual is required to practise ascesis, renunciation, patience, detachment and service.[17] Christian tradition has something similar. Purification is obtained by leaving in God's hands justice which resorts to strong and cruel measures, and the individual Christian is required to be humble and gentle. Thus feelings of anger and revenge can be ascribed to God. When evil is thus transferred into God's hands the individual can keep his innocence. *This double personality factor* is present in both our civic and ecclesiastical social structures, in order that we may 'sin without sinning' and remain innocent as individuals. The means and weapons of violence are progressively taken away from individuals. Within ecclesiastical institutions individuals are required to be poor, obedient, chaste and to seek personal holiness, whereas the Church as an institution is allowed ambiguous behaviour (wealth, pride, envy, conflict, struggle . . .). How difficult it is to bring poverty, humility, service, ascetic detachment to the anonymous structures in which ecclesiastical institutions are expressed! It seems as if the price to be paid for the pursuit of holiness is to invent subjects (or institutions) to carry the weight of sin. Maoism because of its persistent dualism might succeed finally in constructing an historical subject of service—the state as well as the individual which serves—and do away with the dualism which divides people into two subjects, the 'pure' and the 'impure'. The mystery of Christ who took upon Himself the sin of the world demands that we should choose humanity, even to the point of solidarity with particular sinners. The perennial validity of the Old Testament demands that we should not off-load too easily onto others the weight of ambiguity and sin. God is in man and man is in God; they cannot be set against each other so that we might have a place both in the pure zone, God's, and in the impure, man's. Freedom sees the sun and attains purity only after the work of liberation, which must be done by humanity united, and thus always by a mixture of the pure and the impure, so that the Church too is always 'holy and at the same time sinful'. The way in which to carry this weight of sin is not an easy problem.[18] The fact that there has been this resorting to a doubling of the subject (or personality) shows that a solution is possible and we have only to seek it. However, it is beyond the scope of this article to do so. We content ourselves with having shown the need to co-operate in *the construction of a new humanity, as the first subject of liberation* which truly wins the victory over 'the collective inability to love'. This total transcendence is possible only in God. Maoism has not yet glimpsed it; it strives for a total humanism but remains constricted within a limited vision. Christianity cannot afford the luxury of silence about God and remaining bound within the limits of a humanity which is still divided and finite, within a liberation process which is partial and confined to history.

CONCLUSIONS

Christian salvation needs to be 'saved' from divisions. The two aspects of gift (grace) and task (service) as assigned to God and man are often seen as separate. God's incarnation must be taken seriously. It requires that God and man should be united to live for freedom as a gift of God which becomes a gift to our brothers, a gift received and a gift passed on. *The most important problem of the moment* is not to achieve the unity, within the search for salvation, between material and spiritual values, or between personal and social goods. *It is to create a unity between faith and morality, God and man*. Chinese tradition can help us to rediscover Christianity as a 'way', as a harmony between theory and practice, faith in God and service to men. In particular it can help Christianity to discover God's salvation *within the liberation process struggled for by human beings*. God will be discovered or revealed more at the end than at the beginning, because he is hidden and his presence in history is not always apparent. The history of salvation is not only that which derives from an explicit faith, that places God at the beginning. Historical scrutiny which seeks to discern God's initiative in history does not require the proclamation of 'unambiguous' segments of history, enacted by Christians and the Church; otherwise the Old Testament would never have led to Christ. Today it is urgently necessary to follow the Pauline principle: 'All things are yours; and you are Christ's and Christ is God's' (1 Cor. 3:22-3). *God is to be found at the end of a journey* during which man begins to make the world his own. To the extent that human beings become free they can recognise themselves as children of grace, and restore all things to Christ so that Christ can hand them over to the Father. Christianity cannot and should not feel uncomfortable with slow processes, which do not reveal God immediately and clearly. This new way of seeing things was encouraged in 'Lumen Gentium', at the beginning. No. 1 begins by recognising that mankind is already engaged in a process of unification (and thus liberation and salvation), at various levels, technical, cultural and socio-political. And the Church is invited to take part in this process, because in Christ who is the goal and fulfilment of all time, mankind attains the final stage of unity and freedom, eschatological salvation. The process we see going on appears to be merely 'human'. What is important is that it should always remain open to a broader vision, so that it may become Christian and thus God's. The ability to wait is the ability to take part in the history of freedom.

Translated by Dinah Livingstone

Notes

1. For a bibliography on the theme of 'salvation' see *La salvezza cristiana* (Acts of the 6th Congress of the Associazione Teologica Italiana) (Assisi 1975); R. Facelina (ed.) *Liberation and Salvation. Liberation et Salut. International Bibliography* (Strasbourg 1973); E. Garulli, P. Rossano, C. Molari 'Salvezza' in *Nuovo Dizionario di teologia* (Edizioni Paoline 1977) pp. 1397-1438.

2. See C. Vagaggini 'Storia della salvezza' in *Nuovo Dizionario di teologia* (Edizioni Paoline 1977) pp. 1559-1583.

3. See J. Ching 'Per una risposta cristiana all "nuova Cina"' in *Esperienza cinese e fede cristiana* (Bologna 1976) pp. 22-44.

4. On subjectivism see Mao Tse-tung *Selected Works* (Peking 1965; Oxford 1977) Vol. 1; see ibid. for dogmatism and practice.

5. See Mao op. cit. , vol. I, against the metaphysical conception of the world he rejects in particular the classical saying: 'Heaven is immutable and so is the Tao immutable' (p. 331).

6. See R. Faracy 'Il pensiero di Mao e la fede cristiana' in *Esperienza cristiana* . . . (see note 2) pp. 159-199.

7. See the whole of Mao's speech on Contradiction (August 1937), vol. I *Selected Works* (see note 4).

8. A document on 'Justitia et Pax' (10th December 1974, International Day of the Rights of Man) published as 'Documento di lavoro', No. 1, 1975 (Vatican City), stresses this change from the defence of the rights of 'christianitas' to the defence of the rights of 'societas hominum'; see Nos. 13-35 in 'Regno Documenti' 17 (1975) pp. 388 ff.

9. See R. Faracy op. cit. p. 163.

10. See Mao *Selected Works* vol. III.

11. See Mao op. cit. for the famous speech on the Chinese fable 'How Yu Kung moved the mountain'. Mao exclaims: 'We shall also move heaven, and this heaven is nothing other than the people of the whole of China.'

12. See Mao Tse-tung *Little Red Book* (London 1967).

13. This holistic vision was part of the eschatology of Vatican II; see *Lumen Gentium* No. 7, *Gaudium et Spes* No. 39.

14. In the works of Mao there are only about three or four mentions of religion, and always in a political context or with reference to superstition.

15. On the relationship between Mao and ancient Chinese tradition, see P. Rule 'Il maoismo e aperto al trascendente?' in *Esperienze cinese e fede cristiana* (Bologna 1976) pp. 45-66.

16. See Mao *Selected Works* vol. I.

17. See in *Christianity and the New China* (New York 1976) the contributions of J. Charbonnier, L. Trivière 'The new China and the history of salvation' I, pp. 87-112; J. Spae 'Theology and the new Maoist man' I pp. 155-166; D. van Collier 'The new man in China and in Christianity' II pp. 59-70 in *Christianity and the New China* (vols. I and II) (New York 1976).

18. On the Church 'semper purificanda et reformanda', see K. Rahner 'Il peccato nella chiesa' in *La Chiesa del Vaticano II* ed. G. Barauna (Florence 1965) pp. 419-435 commenting on *Lumen Gentium* No. 8 (end of chap. 1).

Claude Geffré

Theology in the Age of China: Evangelisation and Culture

IT IS NOT necessary to be a specialist in Chinese affairs to feel concerned as a theologian by the reality of China. This reality is part of the historical context within which we must try to rethink what has been entrusted to us in the Christian revelation. The massive fact of China, the fact of a world of over 800 million human beings living outside the sphere of influence of a Church which is still identified with the Western world, is a 'sign of the times' which calls for interpretation in the light of the Gospel. And is not the historic creation of a new mode of existence for human beings as individuals and as a group a challenge to a Christian outlook which prides itself on a utopia in which the interest of the individual is subordinated to the interests of all? Whatever the historical, cultural and political causes, is it possible to explain the impermeability of China to Christianity without bringing in the blatant discrepancy between the historical appearance of the Churches and a living of the Gospel aimed at creating a new humanity?

At the same time, however, a closer acquaintance with the People's Republic, especially as illustrated by the rapidity of change since the death of Mao, will prevent the theologian from being too ready to idealise life in China. Some theologians have no hesitation in talking about the new China as a historical realistion of the kingdom of God (*Gesta Dei per Sinienses* . . .).[1] It is of course true that the history of salvation is mysteriously brought to fulfilment in all nations through the ordinary events of their history, but we are well aware of how theologies of history have come to grief in trying to identify as 'signs of the kingdom' events which first have to be understood in terms of their historical causes. Their

significance for salvation, rather than just for liberation, is almost unver-
ifiable.

In the following pages I shall not try to say what role the new China
might have in the divine plan of salvation. Who would be so rash? I would
simply like to show how the encounter of Christianity and China is
stimulating theological research in those areas which are most important
to our contemporary understanding of Christianity. I am thinking in
particular of the relations between Christianity and culture, of the historical particularity of Christianity and of our new understanding of
mission, of the relations between Christianity as a doctrinal message and
as orthopraxy.

1. HOW CAN ONE BE A CHRISTIAN WITHOUT DENYING ONE'S CHINESE IDENTITY?

I shall start with the question put to the participants in the fourth
meeting of CECC (Catholics in Europe Concerned with China) in Paris in
October 1977: 'Is it possible to be a Taoist, a Confucian or a Maoist and
also a Christian?'

The question is a trick question, and even slightly artificial. Ideally it is
no doubt possible to be a Taoist, a Confucian or even a Maoist and at the
same time to live by the Gospel. On the other hand, it is difficult to admit
in the same person the co-existence of a full Taoist or Maoist identity and
a full Christian identity in so far as this entails adherence to a system of
thought (especially if, as in the case of Maoism, this is an ideology as
opposed to a religion) and membership of a specific social group.

However, the question has the merit of raising a real problem, that of
double religious affiliation, a very urgent problem wherever Christianity
is in contact with a dominant major religion. To talk simply in terms of a
double affiliation to Christianity and to a culture is to be content with a
very superficial view. We must accept that in certain societies (I am
thinking of some Asian countries) belonging to the culture coincides with
belonging to the dominant religion. The problem of evangelisation cannot be presented solely in terms of a conflict between two religions
defined abstractly by their most important elements. We must think of it
as a conflict between two cultures. This is even more true when we are
considering the encounter between Christianity and a Chinese culture
shaped by an indissoluble complex of Confucian, Taoist, Buddhist and
Maoist elements.

To the question, 'Can a person be at the same time totally Christian and
totally Chinese?' the reply must be yes, though it must be realised that the
result can only be a new synthesis which cannot be decreed in advance

and which will be the work of the Chinese Christians themselves. Referring to the situation of the Church in Asia generally, Fr M. Zago writes, 'The Church appears as an alien entity, even to those Asians who sometimes know and love Christ; it is a tree that fails to mature and bear fruit; a philanthropic organisation—so worthy of respect—rather than a way to spiritual experience'.[2] A certain impermeability of China to Christianity invites us to reflect on the conditions necessary for a real 'inculturation' of the faith in a foreign mentality in which cultural elements and religious elements are inextricably mixed. Outside the Western world is Christianity not still too often lived as something alien to the religious and cultural identity of the new converts?

To reach a living synthetis able to overcome the double hazard of a dual affiliation and an improper syncretism, we must start by distinguishing the levels of encounter between Christianity and another religion. The encounter may go a very long way on the cultural and ethical level, and even on the level of basic spiritual experience if by that is meant the particular ways in which the experience of the absolute takes shape (meditation, prayer, the understanding of oneself and of the world, the sense of the sacred). The radically new element will be the way in which faith in Jesus Christ organises, ranks and activates elements belonging to a religious tradition different from that of the historical forms of Christianity. Provided that there is a clear awareness of the break resulting from the new structure given to identical elements by an absolutely different centre of reference, it certainly seems possible to be at the same time a Confucian or a Taoist and a Christian. There are reports of forms of 'Christian Buddhism' in some Asian countries which constitute an original synthesis, both in relation to a purely Buddhist tradition and in relation to the Christian tradition with which we are familiar.[3]

Evangelisation means evangelisation of the whole person and respect for the cultural and religious identity of the person to whom the Gospel is proclaimed. The Church would be giving the lie to its catholicity if it were not capable of adopting the cultural and religious values of the people among whom it takes root. Such a process of implantation is the result of a double movement. On the one hand, Christianity has to play the role of a 'critical catalyst' for the ethical, meditative, ascetic and ritual values of the other religious traditions.[4] On the other hand, the witnesses to the Gospel must also be ready to call in question their usual practices and to accept the existence of an otherness which escapes them. 'We have to entrust the Word to others, let it resonate and "take" in their particular cultures, in those areas of their humanity which we do not know. If they receive the Word we have given them into all that constitutes their personal and collective existence, and if that word succeeds in acquiring a meaning at the deepest level of their singularity, they will speak it in their turn in their human languages.'[5] The task is not to proclaim a different Christianity, but, in conformity with the Church's universal vocation, to encourage the conditions for the appearance of a Christianity with different historical features.

To go on talking in terms of double affiliation, to Christianity on the one hand and to another religion or system of thought on the other, is to admit that the Church's mission has to some extent failed; it is to deny the integrating power of the Gospel. Against the background of the encounter between Christianity and the otherness of China, I am tempted to define the relation of Christianity and culture more generally as an inseparable mixture of a break and a creation.

By 'break' I mean that the Gospel is always something new breaking into human ways of thought, imagination and culture. Historically, the Christian kerygma did indeed bring about a break in ancient man's outlook and language. 'Creation' stresses the fact that, in spite of its newness, the only way the Christian message was able to become intelligible was by becoming a part of existing languages and psychologies.

Again today, the Gospel must remain Good News while becoming to some degree a cultural fact. If the language of the faith does not make this effort of acculturation,[6] there is no Gospel event. There is only the 'false scandal' of an alien or outdated cultural vehicle. But equally, if the language of the faith takes the shape of a particular culture completely and loses its own identity, there is also no Gospel event. It is in terms of this dialectic of continuity and break that we must try to imagine what it might be like for the Gospel to be 'inculturated' in a Chinese mentality structured in different ways by Taoism, Confucianism and Maoism.

2. THE ORIGINALITY OF CHRISTIANITY AS A RELIGION

Whatever may be the future possibilities for an encounter, I feel that this searing concern for these two immense continents so remote from each other, Christianity and China (together they make up almost half the human race), leads us to consider the originality of Christianity as a religion. In this connection we can never meditate enough on the exemplary significance of the relation between Judaism and Christianity.

It is well known that the New Covenant inaugurated by Jesus did not result immediately in a new system of worship, a new priesthood and new temples. Even in the moral order, the newness of Christ's teaching is more the radicalisation of what was already present in germ in the Jewish law as the law of love. The radical newness is concentrated in the event of Jesus Christ, with all its unheard-of implications for relations with God and with others. This newness is reflected above all in the new spirit which was able to incorporate a conceptual universe, a vision of the world and of man and a style of life which could retain their old identities.

It was the demands of the mission to the Gentiles which led to a distinction between the contingent Jewish elements and the Gospel message itself. The Jews who had become disciples of Jesus found it normal to go on attending the synagogue, to have themselves circumcised and not to eat certain meats. So much so that the first Christians were not surprised when the new religion established by Christ was called simply 'the Way' (*hodos*): see Acts 9:2. For them it was an extension of the *halakah* in its role as a system of moral, social and religious rules.[7]

All this should convince us of the fundamental historicity of the Christian faith from its birth. It is impossible to reach the substance of the original Christianity without going through a cultural and religious universe, and this in turn is a complex whole within which it is hard to distinguish the contribution of Semitism, of Hellenism, of Philo, of Stoicism. Today as well, there will be no transmission of the Christian message which escapes from this law of historical incarnation. We are always preceded by the event of Jesus Christ which remains the source and reference of all Christian practice. However, the transmission of this event is inseparable from a re-creation because it is always historical, that is, related to specific human practices, whether they be social, moral, religious or just cultural. 'Christianity is *tradition* because it lives by an initial origin which is *given*. But it is necessarily at the same time always *production* because this origin can only be retold historically and by a *creative* interpretation.'[8]

The 'production' of a Chinese Christianity will be an original creation which no theology can describe in advance, but the pressing demands of the incarnation of the Gospel in cultures other than those of the West and even in other religious traditions invite theology to make a fresh effort to rethink the originality of Christianity as a religion.

What are we really talking about when we talk about Christianity? Do we mean the historical translations of the newness of Christianity with which we have been familiar for two millennia, or the new spirit inaugurated by the spirit of Christ? One could go so far as to say that Christ did not found a new religion if by religion is meant a system of symbols, a set of rites, a catalogue of moral prescriptions or a programme of social practices. Christian existence cannot be defined in advance. It exists wherever the Spirit of Christ raises up a new form of being for man individually and collectively. I am tempted to think that the search for a specific Christian identity is misconceived. There is no such thing as a 'species' called Christianity. There is only a 'genus' of Christianity which is hard to define. We can say that there is a Christian way of being human, of loving, of suffering, of working. It is a way of living which cannot be reduced to the statement of faith. This also means that there is a Christian way of being Chinese whether one is in addition Confucian, Taoist or Buddhist. The question whether it is possible to be at the same time a Taoist or a Buddhist and a Christian thus sends us back to a more radical question: What is the most important thing in Christianity? A system of rites, symbols and practices which are the structural elements common to all religions, or the unpredictable power of the Gospel?

In any case, if in some cases evangelisation cannot totally exclude the problem of a double religious affiliation, it is legitimate to find a structural homology between the relation which primitive Christianity maintained with Judaism and the relation which present-day Christianity maintains with the great non-Christian religions. Just because history shows that the relations between Christianity and the other religions have been lived in terms of exclusion this situation is not necessarily normative for the end of the second millennium. We have already mentioned that we know from Asia of examples of 'Christian Buddhism' or 'Christian Hinduism' which are more than examples of lazy syncretism. They are original creations of the spirit of Jesus. Moreover, even in the West, we are only at the beginning of a new style of Christian existence in which membership of the group known as the Church is less important than membership of a particular human group, and in which the dominant culture is no longer that of what is called Christian civilisation.

To end these brief remarks on Christianity as a religion, the coexistence of the Church and the vastness of modern China suggest to me two conclusions which are also theological tasks.

1. The historical attitude of the Church to the great religions, the fact—revolutionary in the full sense—that we have moved from the idea of conquest to the idea of dialogue, imposes on us the duty of rethinking Tertullian's old idea of *praeparatio evangelica*. The economy of God's design must be understood, not only diachronically, but also synchronically. From this point of view it is too simple, and too triumphalist, to say that Christianity is a leaven which has to bring about an *Aufhebung* (a destruction by taking up) of all religious traditions. Doubtless Christianity will always exercise a critical and purifying role, but we must beware of the illusion that cultural values can be retained while religious elements are purged. The Church is faithful to its universal vocation, not by a missionary *conquest* of other religions, but by its Christian *presence* which is the seed and the promise of the new historical creations which will be a Chinese, an Indian, a Japanese, an Arab Christianity, and so on.

2. Secondly we are led to deepen the idea of the uniqueness of Christianity. The ideas of 'religionless Christianity', 'non-ideological Christianity' and 'Christians without a Church' are being used too much

as strategic devices. There is no Christian faith without an ideological translation or without social visibility. We cannot accept the aristocratic position of Karl Barth's 'dialectical theology' which depreciates other religions as 'mere human projections' in comparison with Christianity, which is said not to be a religion on the pretext that the Gospel puts an end to all religion. But, on the other hand, we have still not exhausted the theological intuition which enabled Barth to describe Christianity as a 'religion of grace'.

This means in particular that Christianity is being unfaithful to itself when it absolutises a historical form, a certain institutional and doctrinal product, as a definitive state of the Church of Christ. The Gospel has a critical function not only with regard to other religions but also with regard to the Christian religion. Specifically, this means that in the face of the challenge—both quantitative and qualitative—of other cultures and other religions, the Church can be faithful to its catholicity only by accepting conversion, that is by accepting a serious questioning of its Western mode of expression.

3. CHRISTIANITY'S HISTORICAL PARTICULARITY AND CLAIM TO ABSOLUTENESS

A certain impermeability to Christianity on the part of China invites us to rediscover our awareness of Christianity's historical particularity. The historical form (to be strictly accurate we should say, the various historical forms) taken by Christianity cannot claim to sum up all the creativity in the order of feeling and in the order of values, all the work of men and women of good will to make the world more human. We are often tempted wrongly to claim as achievements of Christianity a number of values which are simply conquests by the human race in the course of its history. Others before us have denounced the covert triumphalism of such terms as 'implicit Christianity', 'anonymous Christians'. If, for example, it is true that China is succeeding in producing a 'new creature' in the shape of a human being living in society, is it not illegitimate to say that this is only an unfolding of what is already contained in Christian morality?

This confirms our view that it is wrong to argue from the absolute character of the Jesus Christ event as the definitive manifestation of the absolute reality of God to the absolute character of Christianity as a historical religion.[9] Just as there is a God beyond the Bible, there is a Christ beyond Christianity. Christianity as a religion does not contain within itself—as a historical reality—the power to save and to perfect other religions. It simply incarnates the salvation which was prophesied and is now made present in the Church. Christianity has no monopoly of

God's action. According to the teaching of Vatican II, grace is offered to all human beings in ways known to God alone. We therefore cannot be content to accept Karl Rahner's view of non-Christian religions as 'anonymous Christianity'.[10] This would presume that one accepted the 'categorical absolute' of Christianity as the only true religion for all mankind.

Theologically, therefore, we are not obliged to make the Church's universal mission depend on the absolute character of Christianity. We prefer instead to develop one of the main themes of the ecclesiology of Vatican II when it declares that 'in Christ' the Church is 'a kind of sacrament of intimate union with God and of the unity of all mankind' (*Lumen Gentium,* 1). The Church must be seen not just as the people made up of those who have been gathered together by the Word uttered in Jesus Christ, but as the sacrament of the presence of God to the whole human race. The Church as a historical reality has no monopoly of the signs of the kingdom. God is greater than his Church and greater than the historical signs by which he has revealed his presence. These signs do not prejudge other unforeseeable signs concerned with the future of humanity. The seed of Christianity scattered in the West has produced a great tree. We know nothing about the unexpected fruits which may be produced by the hidden seed scattered on Chinese soil.

This in no way lessens the need for evangelisation. 'There is no trace in the early Church of boasting, making the religion of Christ absolute or believing that the Church was the only mediator of salvation.'[11] It is also valuable to remember that Christianity can only keep its identity by accepting its particularity. One can only remain oneself by accepting that one is different and so limited. The surest way of winning attention for the specific truth of the Christian message is to present it as a particular message about man. Understanding does not, after all, start from the general, and a universal message attempting to speak to all is in great danger of being trivial.

Nor must we be content, in a legalistic way, to base the need for evangelisation on the Lord's 'missionary commands'. This vital need derives from the very nature of faith in Jesus Christ. The basis of the urgency of mission is not even the desire to get as many people and nations as possible inside the visible Church on the pretext that 'without the visible mediation of the Church' they would be doomed to eternal damnation. Some people have thought that the conclusions of the new theologies of the salvation of unbelievers entitled them to relax the missionary effort. The documents of Vatican II insist both on the possibilities of salvation offered to those who do not know the Gospel (see esp. *Lumen Gentium*, 16) and on the Church's need of mission. 'Though God in ways known to himself can lead those inculpably ignorant of the

Gospel to that faith without which it is impossible to please him (Heb. 11:6), yet a necessity lies upon the Church (see 1 Cor. 9:16), and at the same time a sacred duty, to preach the Gospel' (*Ad Gentes*, 7). Considering the case of those who are ignorant of the Gospel, Fr Congar comments: 'It is their business and God's business. The Church knows only an obligation deriving from its nature.'[12]

These attitudes have become familiar to us. But how are we to hold together the urgency of mission and the gratuitousness of the proclamation of salvation?[13] This ought to lead us to a theological meditation on the gratuitousness of the love of God itself. God wishes to save all human beings, and yet he did not wish to reduce the long period preceding his manifestation in Jesus Christ. At all events, it is legitimate, in view of the challenge presented to the Church by the fact of China, to formulate a few propositions about the current demands of evangelisation.

1. Missionary activity cannot do without witness to Jesus Christ, whether by word or significant actions. In Fr Chenu's fine expression, we have to 'make the Gospel incarnate in time'. Making the Gospel incarnate means not just bearing witness to Jesus Christ; it also means working to transform men and women, individually and collectively, in the spirit of the Gospel.

2. Unlike proselytism, witness does not necessarily mean conversion in the sense of increasing the number of those affiliated to the Catholic Church. It means primarily ensuring the presence of a Church which looks more and more like the universal sacrament of the salvation won in Christ. This Church will therefore be ready to let its contingent historical forms be questioned by other cultural and religious traditions.

3. It would nevertheless be insufficient to say that the Church's mission is limited to the discernment of the implicitly Christian values contained in this or that religion or culture, and so to respecting and deepening these values. Witness to the Gospel must lead to some sort of conversion, but the conversion in question is a conversion of the heart which does not necessarily entail an estrangement on the part of the new disciples of Jesus from their ethnic, cultural and even religious roots. Jesus' practice remains the absolute norm, but as a result of the variety of historical and socio-cultural conditions it is normal for Christian practices to be diverse. We have to learn to articulate the name 'Christian' in the plural.

4. Whether we are concerned with evangelisation in our Christian countries which have become pagan or in cultures remote from Christianity, theologically and pastorally we must give priority to the idea of threshold or stage. In this connection it is desirable to reflect on the fact that the criteria of ecclesiality do not necessarily coincide with the criteria

of visible membership of the Church as a group. In relation to the plenitude of Christian existence, which is eschatological, there is a plurality of partial realisations, both in the order of faith as confessed and in the order of faith as lived. We need to stress here the analogy between the unity of the Church as a body which is always developing and the identity of Christian existence, which is also always developing.

4. THE IDEA OF THE 'WAY' AS A MEETING-PLACE BETWEEN CHRISTIANITY AND CHINESE THOUGHT

Still as part of a search for the stimulus provided to Christian theology by the 'otherness' of China, this last remark on development in Christianity invites us to think finally about the idea of the 'Way' as the point for a fruitful dialogue between Christianity and Chinese thought.

It is impossible to think of Chinese thought without mentioning Lao Tse's *Book of the Way and of Virtue*. On first acquaintance, the Tao can be regarded as a moral way to follow a life-style. In fact, however, as Fr Claude Larré has shown in his recent commentary,[14] the word *tao* denotes a mysterious reality with multiple harmonics. It is as inadequate as the word God to denote the Absolute. It denotes both the 'way of heaven' and the 'way of the saints'. What it is referring to is the reality beyond appearances, beyond knowledge and experience. In the order of human action, the 'Way' has to do simultaneously with mysticism, wisdom and ascesis.

It is fascinating to note the prominence of the metaphor of the 'Way'—with the same breadth of meaning—in Judaeo-Christian texts. In the New Testament, especially in Acts (see 9:2), the word 'way' (*hodos*) denotes the way *par excellence*, the way of life of Jesus' disciples. It brings out in particular the fact that Christianity is part of the extension of the Jewish *halakah*. It would, however, be a notable impoverishment of the idea of Christianity as the way to take 'way' simply as 'moral conduct'. This image of the 'Way' (with all the words associated with it, especially 'exodus' and 'journey') is a key which gives us access to the most original element of Christianity as a religious system. One word which has become very fashionable recently as a term for this original dimension is 'orthopraxy'. It has the advantage of stressing that there is no such thing as a Christian orthodoxy which does not result in a system of action. However, if it is misunderstood, it may involve the danger of an attempt to look for a too quick rapprochement with other religions by leaving the content of the faith on one side.

1. There have been attempts recently to justify a primacy of orthopraxy over orthodoxy by reference to the Johannine formula 'doing the

truth' (see Jn. 3:21). The Johannine expression was seen as providing a biblical basis for a pragmatist conception of truth according to which the only truth is what is effective or verified by action. However, as Fr de la Potterie has well shown, the Johannine 'doing the truth' does not refer to the believer's moral action as a consequence of the faith, but to the very genesis of the faith.[15] Far from appealing to St John to contrast profession of faith and action, we have to say that for him action *par excellence* is the practice of faith itself. So 'Christianity the way' means not just a system of precepts to be followed, but the actual path of faith.

2. The denunciation of a false interpretation of the Johannine 'doing the truth' leaves us all the freer to insist that the word 'orthopraxy' conceals a very profound truth about the essence of Christianity. In its original environment of the Graeco-Roman world, Christianity did not triumph as a religion of truth (*alēthia*) or a mystery religion, but as a religion of love (*agapē*). Of course we must not oppose profession of the faith and action, but it is nonetheless undeniable that Christianity is defined primarily by a certain kind of action, evangelical action, before being defined as knowledge or as acceptance of a corpus of truths. To regard Christianity as a way or as orthopraxy in the search for a dialogue with the Tao involves realising that Christian action is not just the consequence or the field of application of a doctrinal truth already fully formed. Christian action itself not only reveals but also creates new meanings for the content of the Christian message. To act according to the Spirit of Christ is not just to offer new interpretations of the event which is Jesus Christ, but also to produce new historical forms of Christianity according to the time and the place. Such a conception of Christian action is inseparable from an idea of the truth which identifies neither with an original fullness of being nor with one historical form. Truth is rather under the sign of becoming. It is a permanent coming to be. This is what it means to say that biblical truth is eschatological.[16]

Faith in St John's sense is itself a way. Faith can imply a long journey which includes many stages before reaching the adult state, 'the measure of the stature of the fullness of Christ' (Eph. 4:13). And there is an instinct for truth, a faith which precedes explicit faith and which enables us to understand why evangelical action is not the monopoly of those who are members of the Church or profess explicit faith in Jesus Christ. It is possible without knowing it to be already a disciple of Jesus Christ in a religious system other than that of Christianity in its form of a historical religion. That is why it is so difficult to define the specific features of Christianity in terms of doctrinal orthodoxy or even of orthopraxy if this is taken to mean that there is only one correct Christian way. There is a certain way of practising the beatitudes which cannot be defined in advance. The Christian answer is as unpredictable as the Spirit of Jesus, which does not belong to Christians alone. We should not therefore be surprised if we receive lessons in the meaning of the Gospel either from atheists or from those who belong to religions other than Christianity. Jesus said, 'Blessed are those who have not seen and yet believe'. We can say today, 'Blessed are those who did not know and yet live the Gospel'.

We should be pleased that many people can follow Christ's way, practise the *sequela Christi*, before accepting the dogmatic content of Christian faith and even before explicitly recognising Jesus as Lord. Describing Christianity as a way is thus to suggest that it is more than a particular religion defined by dogmas, a system of worship and criteria of membership: it is the property of every man or woman who is journeying towards the light.

Like the New Testament images of the grain, the seed, the leaven, the metaphor of the way is an attempt to indicate that the kingdom of God is essentially something in motion. Does not this give us a possible connection with the vitalist and organicist language of the Tao? Like the kingdom of God, the Tao is at the beginning an almost invisible seed (see Ch. 67: 'All declare my way to be great—But of miserable appearance'). The Tao defines an intermediate area between that of truth and that of the Law. It belongs to life. That is why it is possible to treat the kingdom of God as an equivalent to the Tao.

The richness of this idea of the way gives me my conclusion to all this study of the confrontation between Christianity and the otherness of China. There is a permanent coming to be of the fullness of the Gospel as an eschatological reality, and this is also true of the Church of Christ as a historical entity. Without a reference to the constitutive event which is Jesus Christ, Christianity becomes trivial. But without creativity it stops being a way open to the unforeseeable future. We know nothing about the historical prospects of Christianity in the China of today and tomorrow, but one thing is certain: it will never really take root in Chinese soil unless it is faithful to its nature and becomes again an exodus.

Translated by Francis McDonagh

Notes

1. I am thinking in particular of the study by G. S. Song 'The New China and the History of Salvation. A Methodological Enquiry' in *Christianity and the New China* (Båstad-Louvain 1974) pp. 113-34. For a critical assessment see D. Grasso 'The New China and God's Plan for Salvation' in *The New China: A Catholic Response* (New York 1977) pp. 81-123.

2. M. Zago 'Evangelisation in the Religious Situation of Asia' *Concilium* 114 (1978) p. 72 or p. 73.

3. M. Zago ibid pp. 77 ff.

4. I have taken the expression from Hans Küng *On Being a Christian* (London and New York 1976) p. 112.

5. E. Juguet 'L'évangélisation peut-elle respecter les cultures?' *Etudes* (November 1978) p. 537.

6. In French 'aculturation' and 'inculturation' are used as synonyms, but the more recent word 'inculturation' stresses better the need for the faith to germinate and grow at the heart of cultures.

7. See C. Perrot 'Halakha juive et morale chrétienne: fonctionnement et références' *Ecriture et pratique chrétienne* (Paris 1978) pp. 35-51.

8. C. Geffré 'La crise de l'herméneutique et ses conséquences pour la théologie' *Rev. des Sc. Rel.* 52 (1978).

9. See A. Ganoczy 'The Absolute Claim of Christianity: The Justification of Evangelisation or an Obstacle to It?' *Concilium* 114 (1978) p. 19.

10. Cf. Küng op. cit. pp. 98 and 126.

11. A. Ganoczy op. cit. p. 25.

12. Y. Congar *Principes doctrinaux dans l'activité missionnaire de l'Eglise (Décret Ad Gentes)* (Paris 1967) pp. 214-215.

13. See C. Geffré 'Evangélisation ou dialogue?' *Parole et Mission* 45 (1969), pp. 225-235.

14. Lao Tseu *Tao te King, Le Livre de la Voie et de la Vertu*, French translation by Claude Larré (Paris and Brussels 1977).

15. I. de la Potterie ' "Faire la vérité": devise de l'orthopraxie ou invitation à la foi?' *Le Supplément* 118 (1976) pp. 283-293.

16. P. Gisel *Vérité et histoire. La théologie dans la modernité. Ernst Käsemann* (Paris 1977) pp. 190-196.

Stanislaus Lokuang

How can one be at the same time authentically Chinese and Christian?

THE abbot Lou was a diplomat. He was the first Minister of Foreign Affairs of the Republic of China, and he served three times as Prime Minister. He accepted whole-heartedly the teachings of Confucius, and was a perfect Catholic. He wrote:

'"My conversion is not a conversion, it is a vocation." I have just come upon this entry in my diary for May 23, 1934, and it sums up the religious history of the Chinese politician who has been led by God rather than by himself towards the Holy Catholic Church, the Benedictine Order and the priesthood.

'I am a Confucianist. I was thirteen when I was put in the foreign language school in Shanghai by my father and I have never completed the full course of traditional Chinese studies. What does it matter! I had already been imbued with the intellectual and spiritual tradition of Confucianism, the worship of the All-High, the practice of filial piety, zeal in performing acts of virtue in order better to understand man and to make practical progress towards the acquisition of virtue, everything that goes to make up the soul of the Chinese race.

'The Confucianist spirit prepared me to see the evident superiority of Christianity, just as it had done the same for Minister of State Paul Zi three centuries ago, and that in spite of the personal deficiencies of Christians, or rather at the very level of the qualities and deficiencies of man. The Confucianist spirit prepared me to recognise the quite evident superiority of the Holy Roman Church which possesses a treasure from which the believer can draw out values old and new from century to century, a living treasure which grows and fructifies from age to age.'[1]

In the quotation given above, there is mention of Paul Zi. He was a disciple of Matteo Ricci, and has been considered as one of the apostles of China. He was also a Prime Minister of the Empire, and he affirmed 'that the doctrine of Christ could complete and perfect Confucian doctrine, and modify Buddhism'.[2]

The late President Chiang Kai-shek, who died some years ago, wrote in his last will and testament: 'I have, at all times, considered myself a disciple of Jesus Christ and a follower of Dr Sun Yat-sen.'[3]

I have quoted the sayings of these three illustrious Chinese, to demonstrate that an authentic Chinese can be an authentic Christian.

An authentic Chinese must have a deep esteem for matters of the spirit. He must respect Heaven and his Ancestors. He must observe the Confucian moral code. He must cultivate the five virtues of charity, justice, temperance, fidelity and prudence. He must have filial piety to build family.

An authentic Christian must love God above all things, and his neighbour as himself. He must observe the Ten Commandments. He must put eternal life as the final aim of his life.

When we compare the conditions of these two types of life, we find that they are not contradictory to one another. They reciprocally complete one another.

He who lives out filial piety, and considers the well-being of parents as the most important duty of life, will better understand the filial devotion that is due to the Heavenly Father, and will imitate the filial piety of Jesus Christ for His Father.

He who is accustomed to Confucian love for all men, will better experience the all-embracing charity of Christ.

He who lives according to the teaching of Mencius, preferring justice to his own life, will better follow Christ in his sacrifice of himself for the sake of justice.

During the beginnings of evangelisation in China, Matteo Ricci saw clearly that a Chinese who is converted to Christianity would be able to be true to his personal identity. After the question of the Chinese Rites, missionaries obliged new Chinese Christians to abandon their traditions. Later, the Western powers tried to dominate China, through colonialism. As a consequence, the Catholic religion became considered as a foreign religion, and the Christians as instruments of Western powers. This regrettable situation gradually changed. When Pope Pius XI, in 1922, sent the first Apostolic Delegate to China, in the person of Monseignor Celso Constantini, the latter studied Chinese traditions and grew in appreciation of them. It was he who introduced the study of Chinese literature in the seminaries, where before the study of Latin had been the major concentration.

Since Vatican Council II, the principle of establishing the local church has been accepted in China and all over the world. In Formosa, we are studying Chinese tradition, Chinese philosophy and Chinese religions, with the intention of establishing our church in Chinese culture, so that the Catholic Church in China will no longer give the impression of being a foreign religion, and every Chinese Catholic can identify himself as an authentic Chinese.

However, if we consider a Chinese person living under communism, and ask the question whether an authentic Chinese can also be an authentic Chinese Christian, the answer cannot be the same.

But, first of all, we must ask whether a Chinese living under communism can really be an authentic Chinese. The principles of communism are the principles of Marxism. Communist policy is patterned according to communist policy in Soviet Russia. The Chinese Communist Party forced the people of Mainland China to deny their own traditions, as well as Confucian philosophy. They first broke up the family, and destroyed the children's filial piety for their parents. Secondly, they educated them to mutual hatred and mutual conflict. Thirdly, they abolished all forms of religious beliefs, and forbade the worship of Heaven and of ancestors. Fourthly, they used materialism as the explanation of everything. Furthermore, they used materialistic thought to alter the content of Chinese history, thus upsetting all the values of human life. Consequently, a Chinese who is forced to submit to the communist model of life can no longer be a traditional Chinese.

Chinese people living according to the communist model of life for man definitely cannot be authentic Christians either. They may live as poor a life as Jesus Christ did. They may suffer persecution for the sake of justice. They may justify class struggle for the sake of social justice. They may consider national liberation as a fight for human rights. But, all of this together does not fully express the genuine meaning of the Christian gospel. Why is this so? Because within the tenets of materialism, they cannot assert that God exists. They cannot accept Jesus Christ as the Saviour of mankind. They cannot keep in contact with the Roman pope, who is the successor of the apostle Saint Peter. The Catholic believers of mainland China can only keep their faith within their inner hearts; they cannot give it outward expression. They can be compared with the Christians of the catacombs of ancient Rome. Even if the communists allow them to give expression to their faith openly, they still do not recognise or admit their belief in a spiritual God. Presently, the Catholics of Poland are opposing the communist party in their country. They refuse to accept communist principles, and thus they keep their identity as authentic believers. The Catholics in mainland China do not have the same opportunity as do the Catholics in Poland, who openly oppose the communists. They can only fight an inner spiritual battle, with the hope that they ever remain a little more true to their Christian belief. The 'liberation' of Mao Tse-tung has no theological meaning, only Darwin's theory of the survival of the fittest. What Mao Tse-tung advocated for the proletariat has not one iota of the spirit of Christ, nor of the real meaning of social justice, except for a period of historical dialectical materialism. If you give a theological explanation to the above thinking, the result will only be a partial, unilateral theological illusion. If you think that such an explanation can represent the religious concepts of a Chinese Catholic in mainland China, then their religious belief can no longer be considered as authentic Christian belief.

Notes

1. Dom Pierre-Celestin Lou Tseng-tsiang *Souvenirs et pensées* (Desclée pp. 94, 97).

2. Stanislaus Lokuang *The Life of Paul Zi* (Taipei 1970) p. 17.

3. *Tribute to President Chiang Kai-shek*, Commemorating the Third Anniversary of His Passing (Taipei 1977).

Edmond Tang

Can one be truly Christian and Chinese at the same time? —Point of view of a Christian from Hong Kong

THE CHINESE CONVERSION EXPERIENCE

MY task is straightforward. I shall try to draw your attention to how a Chinese convert to Christianity tends to see the question before us. This is already to take up a certain stand. Instead of standing at a distance comparing China and Christianity in their similarities and differences, I am adopting the attitude of someone deeply involved with both and living in the constant tension that relates the two.

As I see it, our problem comprehends at least three levels of activity. There is first of all the psychological level. The conversion of an individual can be seen as a search for a new ego-ideal in Christianity. The old one is somehow lost or found to be inadequate. Consequently it always implies a certain amount of moral conflict. Christian conversion is the breaking in of Jesus Christ, in the form of a person or a cultural system depending on the case, which produces a new hierarchy of personal values and orientations.

It is precisely in the re-arrangement of personal orientations that we become aware of a second level of activity. Inner conversion is always accompanied by a change of attitude towards a particular social group or national tradition. This is evident especially in the conversions that take place in Asian countries where a homogeneous religious and political tradition used to dominate. How conversion takes place and what a person is converted to depend on how and in what form Christianity enters the person's social world—i.e., as a dominant, superior cultural

92

system, or as the subversive power of the eschatology of an oppressed people. The movement of the Jewish diaspora into the dominant Hellenic world and the colonial activities of the Middle Ages have produced very different conversions.

There is a third level of activities, which is the effort of the convert to reconstruct his symbolic universe. He is then operating with existing theological models or trying to find new ones to accommodate his experience and project his future. A new ideological basis is to be found for an indigenised community of faith. It is important to stress again here that the success or failure of this enterprise is very much related to the working out of the social and psychological factors in the conversion experience and its development.

The Chinese Christian's conversion experience can sometimes be compared to a seven-year itch. He is someone born into an arranged marriage with his cultural tradition. But that culture was disintegrating over the last hundred years because of internal corruption and the introduction of Western capitalism. It was no longer capable of satisfying the Chinese who came into contact with the West with any consistent world-view or identity. Christianity entered China at this particular moment with the freshness and charm of European liberal ideas and material progress. She at once captured the hearts of many Chinese, who then became Christians. Some of them have since then arranged a divorce with their own cultural identity; others continue to live in this 'abnormal' situation until today. Then all of a sudden, the China rejected by the Chinese Christian came out of her depression and recovered her pride and beauty among the nations of the world and rekindled in the Chinese Christian a new admiration and love that had never been entirely lost. At the same time his conversion to Christianity became a source of shame and a sign of his infidelity.

What wise counsel can a good pastor give? Pauline privilege? Maintenance of the 'adulterous' situation as the only possible solution in the circumstances? Or, to push the imagery still further, if Christianity claims the capacity of transcending cultures, might not her role be that of the 'lover' of the world? This last remark may sound a little vulgar, but is it not possible to imagine Christianity as a once-and-for-all extra-marital experience that serves to bring about a deeper relationship between the estranged spouses, so that in discovering Christianity the disloyal Christian is sensitised to the real beauty and value of his neglected culture? There is a certain similarity between this latter way of thinking and some contemporary missiological approaches, which consider that the main aim of mission is not to draw heathen souls into the saving institutions of Christianity, but to make Buddhists better Buddhists, or Marxists better Marxists, in a word human beings more human.

THE NEED TO COME TO TERMS WITH HISTORY

Chinese Christians who have arrived at a personal synthesis between their faith and their culture have not been lacking. There were Catholics known to the West such as Dom Pierre-Célestin Lou or John Wu. Both developed a spirituality that drew its richness from Chinese philosophical traditions. However, their theologies were strictly orthodox—i.e., Western—and did not reflect at all the violent social struggles going on in the China of their time. Their main weakness, as well as that of their Protestant counterparts, lies in their basically idealist philosophy—the fact that China was understood only culturally and not socially, and that they did not come to terms with that part of history which still haunts the Chinese Christian today.

If there is any lesson to be drawn from the Chinese revolution in our context, it is that historical wrongs are rarely forgotten. This is simply because history is the memory of a people and does not belong to any one individual or generation. The Chinese communists, part of whose programme is to rid China of all traces of foreign domination, has kept Chinese history jealously apart. It does not matter how the Christian would like to see it: the result of the last hundred years is that there are two antagonistic histories, that of China and of the Christian West, and the separation is almost total.

Some Christians in the West would have it that the two histories are really one. Some have gone as far as extending the biblical umbrella to the Chinese Long March, etc. Admirable as an exercise of broadmindedness, it has hardly struck a sympathetic chord in the Chinese heart. The difficulty is to be found in their assumption of a sort of salvation-history theology. This kind of theology still conceives history as idealist, suprahistorical; it rarely goes beyond the repetition of biblical categories. It is quite all right for Western Christians to talk about the God of their Fathers, since they have never been subjugated in the name of that God. For a Chinese to do the same amounts to calling on the ancestors of an alien tribe. For all practical purposes nothing has really changed; the bridge between the two histories does not yet exist.

IN SEARCH OF A 'KAIROS' IN HONG KONG

The compatibility of Christianity with the Chinese tradition is a question of historical praxis—whether historical divisions can come together again. This has been borne out by the experience of a new generation of

Christians in Hong Kong, for whom the problem of China and Christianity goes beyond the usual dialogue of minds. What is special to them is the close relation between their commitment to China and their commitment to the society in which they find themselves. Not only are they aware of the fact that the future of Hong Kong will be determined by that of China, but their involvement in the society of Hong Kong is the necessary foothold they must gain, and the proof they must furnish, in order to participate in the history of China's tomorrow. At the same time it is impossible for them to conceive their involvement in Hong Kong without reference to China. Social action always implies alliances and oppositions, and it brings them shoulder to shoulder with other groups for whom China is not only a source of inspiration, but also the ideological framework within which they work out their strategies for Hong Kong.

A process of rethinking their Christianity has begun and it has begun by leaving Western church structures and bourgeois mentalities which do not relate to the poor or their commitment to the poor. This movement down to the base is seen as an essentially purifying process, a self-emptying that has become the reason for as well as the way of being Christian today. This has two implications for our problem. Firstly, it carries the salvation-history theologies a step further: it was discovered that God did not only take part in history but that he took sides as well. Secondly, this class commitment contributes to the creation of a new universalism of the oppressed. The incarnation is to be situated more in the history of class than in that of race or nation, with a view to a society in which class too will be superseded. In relation to this China will hopefully not be a jealous rival but a potential participant.

How far a Chinese Christianity will emerge from this experience depends on how this new universalism will supersede historical memories and divisions, and on whether it will lead to a viable theology of incarnation and of history. The Chinese Christian will probably remain Chinese, with his Confucian humanity, Taoist interiority, Buddhist compassion, etc. But he will no longer be a Chinese apart. All these elements will be carried forth in the search of a particular 'kairos' when China and Christianity will find themselves partners in making history one.

Donald MacInnis

The Churches in New China

FOR several reasons it is difficult to write about the churches in New China. In the first place, it is presumptuous for anyone but a Chinese Christian participating in the church in China to attempt to report and interpret the life of that church. There is very little information available to us about the church in China today: neither the Protestant nor Catholic national church organisation publishes statistics, reports, or journals. Second, although recent visitors have talked with some church leaders, and Chinese visitors from abroad have visited Christian friends and relatives at village and neighbourhood level, we have no overall picture by which to appraise the vitality of local Christian congregations, their outreach in the larger community, and theological developments during these years. Finally, there is always the problem of personal bias and worldview. The Christian observer from the West, conditioned by his religious, cultural and political orientation, seeks familiar landmarks to find his way in an unfamiliar socio-political landscape.

Then what can be said about the church in new China? What sources of information are there, and can they be interpreted objectively? The answer is that there are considerable data on the churches and religion from the first fifteen years of this period. The Protestant journal *Tien Feng* was published up to 1964.[1] A series of articles on theories of religion appeared in several national journals including *People's Daily, Red Flag* and *New Construction* as late as 1964-65; and the Forum of Confucian Scholars in 1962 was widely reported in the Chinese press.[2] But the Cultural Revolution (1966-71) disrupted religious practice, as it did all aspects of life and culture, and the Chinese press has published very little on religion since then.

As for unofficial and unpublished information about the churches since that time, there are numerous reports from overseas Chinese who have visited their friends and families in China, reports from Chinese Christians who have emigrated to Hong Kong or overseas, and information gleaned from recent interviews with church leaders inside China, such as K. H. Ting, the president of Nanking Theological College, Wu Yi-fang, former president of Ginling Christian Women's College and with certain Catholic, Protestant and Moslem priests, nuns, pastors and imams.[3] Even so, we have only scattered impressions of the church in China today.

Finally, the situation of the Christian church and other religions in China today must be understood in the overall socio-political context of contemporary China, a nation undergoing extraordinary change and development, its leaders committed to socialist nation-building guided by a totally secular ideology. Under the concept of the United Front, religious believers who serve the nation like other citizens have full citizens' rights; religious leaders from each of the major religions serve in the National People's Congress and other organs of government at provincial, municipal and local levels. Yet China is a fully secularised nation today; the practice of religion is marginal, a private exercise considered irrelevant to the main events in China's drive for modernisation by the year 2000.

RELIGIOUS POLICY IN THE PEOPLE'S REPUBLIC OF CHINA

To speak of the Christian churches in China today, one must speak of all religions, and of the official policy toward religion, as well as the implementation of that policy through various periods since 1949. Moreover, one needs to understand how religion is defined in China today, the distinctions between religion and superstition, and the variations in official policy toward different religions and different functions of religion. Finally, it should be noted that periods of repression of the religious rights of believers at the local level have coincided with intensive national political campaigns designed to mobilise the people for specific goals, such as the anti-rightist campaign in 1957-58 and the Cultural Revolution, 1966-71.

Article 88 of the Constitution of the People's Republic of China pledges that 'Every citizen of the People's Republic of China shall have freedom of religious belief'. The revised constitution adopted in 1975 qualifies that pledge by adding two conditions: 'All citizens of the People's Republic of China shall have freedom of religious belief; they also have freedom not to believe, and freedom to propagate atheism.'

No attempt is made in the Constitution, or in any other legislative or executive document to define religion, or to prescribe the limits of religious belief and practice. 'Freedom of religious belief' evidently can be interpreted by local officials as broadly or as narrowly as they believe appropriate. However, through the years the functions of institutional religion were increasingly restricted until during the Cultural Revolution virtually the only religious practice known was the informal convening of groups of believers for worship.

At the same time, clear distinctions were made between religions and superstitions; the latter were declared non-religious, therefore outside the constitutional guarantee of freedom of religious belief. According to Ya Han-chang, a Marxist theoretician writing in *Hsin Chien-she* (New Construction) in 1964; 'Feudal superstitions, though having their organisations, groups, and activities, have no religious doctrine and do not have the characteristics of religion. Feudal superstition is not religion.'[4] For Ya Han-chang, feudal supersititions include ancestral worship, sorcery, exorcism, fortune-telling, physiognomy, geomancy, worship of local gods, and the activities of the secret societies. Because of their socially non-productive and exploitative nature 'all these activities must be repressed' and their practitioners made to reform and 'earn an honest living'.

Religion, by which Ya means the developed religions with organised activities and doctrine, is quite different; he clearly advocates a 'democratic' policy towards religious believers, citing Chairman Mao's injunction in his 'On Correct Handling of Contradictions Among the People': 'We cannot destroy religion by an administrative order or force people not to believe in religion. . . . The only way to settle questions of an ideological nature or controversial issues among the people is by the democratic method, the method of discussion, of criticism, of persuasion and education, and not by the method of coercion or repression.'[5]

But advocating the rights of religious believers does not imply endorsement of religion as a legitimate belief. In 1940 Mao Tse-tung wrote, 'communists may form an anti-imperialist and anti-feudal united front for political action with certain idealists and even with religious believers, but we can never approve of their idealism or religious doctrines'.[6] The standard view of religion is derived from the writings of Marx and Engels. In an essay published in 1938, Mao wrote: 'The history of science furnishes man with proof of the material nature of the world and of the fact that it is governed by laws, and helps man to see the futility of the illusions of religion and idealism and to arrive at materialist conclusions.'[7]

The official policy toward religion through the years has been, despite the unofficial fluctuations during periods of high political activity, a policy of toleration toward religious believers while holding adamantly to the Marxist rejection of religion as a legitimate belief system. The Religious

Affairs Bureau of the United Front Department, through its national, provincial and local branches, transmits official policy and correlates religious activities through national associations organised by each of the major religions.

Policy toward the three recognised religions—Buddhism, Islamism, and Christianity—has varied through the years. After a virtual black-out of news about religious activities during the Cultural Revolution (1966-71), all three religions have appeared in Chinese news releases from time to time in recent years. Delegations of Buddhists from Japan, for example, have visited China several times in recent years, reciprocated in 1978 by a Chinese Buddhist delegation to Japan.[8] Similar delegations from Moslem countries have been reported in the Chinese press.

However, no groups representing the Christian churches of other nations have entered China since the mid-1950s, nor have Chinese church leaders attended any international church conferences outside China since that time. The reasons for these differences among the three religions are complex, involving China's relations with third world nations as against the Western nations, the residual resentment of Christian missions as a form of cultural imperialism, and the policy of *tzu li keng sheng* (self-reliance) in every aspect of socialist nation-building which abjures dependence on foreign aid or foreign models of any kind.

SELF-RELIANCE AND THE CHURCHES

The policy of self-reliance and nation-building by developing indigenous models has been reflected in the history of the Christian churches. The first stage in reorganisation of the churches was to implement the 'three-self' model, first articulated in the *Christian Manifesto* of May 1950, signed by 400,000 Protestant Christians:[9] self-support, self-propagation and self-government. This required the complete severance of dependence on missionary leadership and foreign funds. By early 1951 the missionaries had either left the country or were waiting for exit permits, and the Edict of December 29, 1950 following the freezing of funds by the American government due to the Korean War, had cut off all outside financial support for the Chinese churches. This was the first stage in the reorganisation of the churches.

The second stage, the merging of Protestant denominational efforts into a single organisation, began with the Three-Self Reform Movement, initiated by 151 church leaders at a meeting in Peking in April 1951 called by Premier Chou En-lai. In the *United Declaration of Chinese Christian Churches*, the conference delegates called upon Chinese Christians '. . .

to thoroughly, permanently and completely sever all relations with American missions and all other missions, thus realising self-government, self-support and self-propagation in the Chinese church'.[10] They also pledged to support the government's land reform policy, the *Common Programme*, to obey all laws, to exert every effort in reconstruction of the nation, and 'to assist the government to discover and punish anti-revolutionary and corrupt elements within the Protestant church'. It was at this time that all church-related schools, hospitals and social service institutions were placed under provincial, municipal or other secular control and administration.

The last of the National Christian Conferences (up to this writing) was held in Shanghai in 1961, with 319 delegates. Dr Wu Yi-fang, former president of Ginling Christian Women's College, presented the executive committee's report, summarising the work of the organisation since the 1954 conference, the state of the theological schools and Christian publishing agencies, and the participation of pastors and laity in the socialist education programme, thereby 'increasing our sense of unity with the people'.[11]

THE INDIGENOUS CHURCHES

Leaders of the Three-Self Movement came primarily from the churches founded by the major mission societies, thereby linked historically to the parent denominations in Europe and North America. Another important sector of the Chinese church was founded and organised completely by Chinese clergy and laity. Each of these indigenous churches was known for its vitality, its independence of all foreign support or leadership, and its distinctive identity and theology. The best known of these were the Jesus Family, the True Jesus Church and the Little Flock (literally, the Assembly Places). In addition there were well-known pastors of independent congregations, such as Wang Ming-tao of the Christian Tabernacle in Peking. Because they did not join the Three-Self Movement these groups and their leaders were seen as dissidents and deprived of their right to continue independently.

THE CATHOLIC CHURCH

The Roman Catholic Church in China, with a history of three and a half centuries, numbered between two and three million members in 1949— three to four times the number of Protestants. Because they were unified in a single Church and ecclesiology under a hierarchy that extended all the way to Rome, they received special attention from the new leadership. The movement for the 'Three Autonomies' was pressed by the Religious Affairs Bureau for several years until the National Patriotic Catholic Association was formed in 1957, with Archbishop P'i Shu-shih as chairman—the same Archbishop P'i who attended the Chinese People's Political Consultative Conference (CPPCC) in February 1978 bearing the title of chairman of the Chinese Catholic Patriotic Association.

The Catholic churches went through a pattern of curtailment and attenuation similar to the Protestant experience, with the notable exception of the Chinese hierarchy. Over forty bishops were elected and consecrated during this period without endorsement from the Vatican, which considers them illicit but not schismatic. According to a Chinese priest residing in France, the new prelates are not schismatic because they 'act in good faith solely with the pastoral intention of preserving the Church and protecting their flocks'.[12]

VILLAGE CHURCH LIFE

What do we know of Christian life at the village level? Judging by numerous first-hand reports from various provinces, Christians meet together regularly for worship. A young Chinese Christian who came to Hong Kong in 1976, and has occasionally returned to her home village, was interviewed in 1978:[13]

Question: Most people will be surprised to learn that you are a Christian. Most post-Cultural Revolution accounts of life in China suggest Christians in China have been effectively suppressed.
Miss Wong: I can't speak about other areas, but in my own village this is not true. I was only a small girl during the Cultural Revolution but then, as now, my family regularly joins in house worship and Bible study.

Question: During this time did your family or village suffer any difficulties from government authorities?
Wong: As far as I know, no one in our village suffered. We're only simple peasant farmers. Why should we have been harmed? In fact, some of the local cadres are also Christian. . . .

Question: Can you say something about your worship services?
Wong: We meet regularly in people's homes. We observe Saturday as the Sabbath and normally do not work that day. People attend various house meetings whenever they are free and interested. Usually there is a meeting in someone's home every night. Our services include singing, praying, reading Scripture and preaching. Everyone is expected to share

in these activities. We don't have persons designated for one particular job.

Recently about one hundred people in our area were baptised. . . . Regarding the Lord's Supper, we celebrate it quite often. We use a traditional order of worship. This is very important to us.

Question: As a Christian living in a socialist land, how do you relate your faith to love for your country?

Wong: Well, I'm Chinese and of course I love my country. I am not a member of the Party but I support my nation. We have a saying in our Church, 'Love country, love the Lord and love peace'. I see no contradiction in this, do you?

CONCLUSION

Despite a pervasive secularism and an unremitting ideological hostility to all religions, both official and unofficial reports confirm that the churches survive in new China. Under the new political leadership the disgraced 'Gang of Four' are blamed for 'undermining the enforcement of religious policy' (freedom of religious belief). More churches have opened their services to foreign visitors. Some Buddhist temples and monasteries with functioning clergy have been opened to foreign visitors.

Religious studies are being resumed, according to recent visitors' reports, with students enrolled in both Catholic and Protestant theological studies. More than one hundred persons attended a forum on religious research, held in Peking, April 10-11, 1978. The forum was chaired by Jen Chi-yu, head of the Institute for Research on World Religions, established in 1964 on instructions from Chairman Mao but evidently not implemented until 1978, when students were enrolled 'to conduct serious and scientific study of world religions', including Buddhism, Christianity, Islam and Taoism.[14]   Finally, after being absent from national news reports since the early 1960s, sixteen prominent Roman Catholic, Protestant, Buddhist and Moslem leaders were listed among the delegates attending the Chinese People's Political Consultative Conference in February 1978, and identified by the organisation they represented. Mentioned were the Chinese Catholic Patriotic Association, the All-China Conference of Protestant Churches, and the Islamic and Buddhist Associations of China.[15]

These are straws in the wind. Only time will tell if religious practice will be restored to pre-Cultural Revolution levels. But the new leadership is breaking precedents in so many ways that a more vigorous implementing of Mao Tse-tung's injunction in *On Coalition Government* (1945) can be expected: 'All religions are permitted . . . in accordance with the principle of freedom of religious belief. All believers . . . enjoy the protection of the people's government so long as they are abiding by its laws. Everyone is free to believe or not to believe: neither compulsion nor discrimination is permitted.'[16]

Notes

1. See *China Bulletin* (1949-64), East Asia Office, National Council of Churches of Christ in the USA (NCCCUSA), New York, for translations from *Tien Feng*.

2. Selections reprinted in D. MacInnis *Religious Policy and Practice in Communist China* (New York 1972), Section 3, 'Theoreticians Debate Religious Policy, Theory and Tactics'.

3. Reports in *China Notes* (NCCCUSA); *Information Letter* (Marxism and China Study, Lutheran World Federation, Geneva); *China Talk* (China Liaison Office, United Methodist Church, Hong Kong); *China Study Project Bulletin* (British Council of Missionary Societies); *Echange France-Asie Dossier* (26, rue de Babylone, Paris); *Pro Munda Vita Reports* (Brussels); *Mondo e Missione* (Pontificio Istituto Missioni, Milan), etc.

4. 'On the Difference Between the Theist Idea, Religion, and Feudal Superstition' *Hsin Chien-she* (New Construction), Feb. 20, 1964, in MacInnis op. cit. p. 48.

5. 'On the Correct Handling of Contradictions' (1957) in MacInnis op. cit. p. 13.

6. 'On Religion and the United Front' (1940) in MacInnis op. cit. p. 12.

7. 'Dialectical Materialism: Notes of Lectures at K' ang-chan ta-hsueh' (*War of Resistance University Magazine* April 1938), in MacInnis op. cit. pp. 10-11.

8. 'Buddhist Describes Life in China' *Japan Times,* May 18, 1978.

9. 'The Christian Manifesto: Direction of Endeavour for Chinese Christianity in the Construction of New China' in *Documents of the Three-Self Movement* Francis P. Jones, editor, Far Eastern Office, NCCCUSA, New York, 1963, p. 19.

10. Chinese text in *Tien Feng*, May 8, 1951; translated in *China Bulletin* Vol. I, No. 108.

11. 'The Second General Conference of the Three-Self Movement' in *Tien Feng,* January-February 1961; translated in *Documents of the Three-Self Movement* p. 194.

12. Fr Wei Tsing-sing 'Open Letter to the West' *Commonweal*, Nov. 25, 1966, pp. 222-25; cited in R. Bush *Religion in Communist China* (Abingdon, New York and Nashville 1970) p. 146.

13. 'Christian Worship in Rural China' interview in *China Talk*, China Liaison Office, United Methodist Church, Hong Kong; cited in *China Study Project Bulletin* No. 6 (1978) op. cit.

14. *Hsinhua,* New China Daily News Release, March 1, 1978.

15. Ibid.

16. 'On Coalition Government' (1945), cited in D. MacInnis op. cit. p. 14.

Jean Charbonnier

Chinese Christianity outside China

ABOUT twenty-two million Chinese live outside the land of their ancestors. This figure does not include Taiwan, which is a Chinese province, or Hong Kong, which is the commercial centre of South China and is under British rule. For the most part, the overseas Chinese (*Hua ch'iao*) do not have Chinese nationality. Many are still stateless, but they are tending more and more to become citizens of the countries in which they live. They are scattered over 115 countries in all five continents. The great majority are concentrated in South-East Asia.

1. FROM COOLIE TO BANKER: AN EVENTFUL HISTORY

In spite of the economic success of certain families, overseas Chinese have led, and in some cases still lead, a precarious existence. Today's businessmen and teachers often had a great-grandfather who was a starving peasant, who left his own country to save his family from dire poverty. Transported in ships' holds to unknown lands, the first Chinese migrants were employed on the most arduous tasks, such as clearing the virgin forest of Malaysia, or building the trans-continentl railway line in the United States. Patient and docile, like new slaves, they were nevertheless able to organise themselves. They were also the custodians of a long cultural tradition of which their language held the secret. Exploited, ill-treated, subjected to pogroms, they managed nevertheless to survive. They won friends in all countries through the efficiency with which they

104

worked and the growing importance of their contribution to the economy.

The long history of the Chinese migrants is not finished, although most countries have now closed their doors to immigration. These migrants constitute ethnic minority groups which still suffer on occasion from discriminatory measures. In some cases the purchase of land or the practice of certain professions is forbidden. They have no other alternative but to become traders, despite the contempt with which Chinese tradition has always regarded such activities. They have excelled in trading, it is true, for very many years. The network of Chinese chambers of commerce and banks in South-East Asia has become a source of prosperity for the local economy.

2. A COMMUNITY RECEPTIVE TO CHRISTIANITY

For centuries past, there have been some members of the Chinese diaspora who have accepted Christianity. In Manila in 1661, the Spanish Dominicans gathered together a community of 4,000 Chinese Catholics. From the middle of the nineteenth century, the great Chinese migrations into South-East Asia and America encountered the full force of the Christian missionary expansion. Communities were formed in Singapore and Malaysia among the various dialect groups. Being a Christian allowed one to aspire to a more open form of education, and made for easier relations with foreign traders and administrators. Towards the end of the nineteenth century, the young Sun Yat-Sen discovered the Christian faith in an Anglican school in Honolulu. In those regions of Central America in which Chinese coolies had replaced the former slaves, the Christian faith was a means of attaining a higher status in the local society. Christian priests such as Father François Tam Assou in Cholon (1897), Father Chiang in Réunion (1890) or Father Philippe Lau in New Guinea in about 1930, played an active part in the development of Catholic communities. When the People's Republic of China was established in 1949, Catholics represented about 2 per cent of a diaspora which at that time numbered ten million Chinese.

3. THE FURTHERANCE OF A SPECIFICALLY CHINESE APOSTOLATE

In the next twenty years, this proportion rose to 3 per cent, whereas the total population of the diaspora doubled. Catholics numbered 750,000 in

1978. Including the Protestants, the percentage of Christians reached 5 per cent, or ten times as many as in China itself. Various surveys have analysed the process of conversion in the fifties and sixties. The rapid changes in social life caused the ghettoes to explode. The extended family broke up into smaller units. Traditional ideals were threatened. Many Chinese entered the local Catholic community because of their need for security and fraternal solidarity as well as to find a new basis for their traditional ideal of man.

This movement benefited from the support of priests, monks and nuns, whether missionaries or Chinese, who could no longer serve in China itself. Many of them, it is true, flooded into the island of Taiwan with the two million or so refugees from the mainland. Some settled in Hong Kong, where they developed many agencies to aid refugees and also many educational bodies. Far too many were transferred to work outside the Chinese diaspora, thus losing the benefit of their experience of China. The attention of the Church had to be drawn to the importance of the diaspora as such. The Bishop of Ninghsia, Mgr Carlo Van Melckebeke, expelled from China in 1952, was to devote himself, body and soul, to this task.

In May 1953 the Congregation of the Propagation of the Faith named Mgr Van Melckebeke Apostolic Visitor of the overseas Chinese. His mission was to further and to co-ordinate the apostolate among the overseas Chinese, without, however, having any particular power of jurisdiction. One of his most urgent tasks was to ensure that the 200 or so young Chinese priests who had been studying in seminaries abroad at the time of the Communist seizure of power in their country were placed in the most appropriate posts. He was later to provide for the renewal of the clergy by encouraging the founding of two small Chinese seminaries at Phulam, near Saigon, and Cébu in the Philippines.

Whilst dealing with the most urgent needs, he also put together the elements of a specific and permanent mission. In Singapore, which contains the greatest concentration of Chinese outside China, he founded a Central Catholic Bureau whose outreach very rapidly became worldwide. The Bureau includes a publicity department, a bookshop, a system of religious instruction by correspondence course, a catechetical service and a Prayer Union for China. It offers financial support to all agencies contributing to the progress of the Chinese Christian communities. Aware of the necessity of developing a specifically Chinese understanding of Catholicism, the Apostolic Visitor encouraged the founding of two study centres in 1957: the Studium Sociologicum of Singapore, run by the Franciscans, to disseminate the social teaching of the Church in the setting of South-East Asia and China; and the Studium Sinicum at Königstein in Germany, set up as a centre for publishing and information.

The first of these centres which might have had a promising role for the future, was unfortunately to be later transplanted to Taiwan.

Lastly, social and financial help is given to displaced persons and refugees. This mutual aid service is well suited to the mobile society of the diaspora. The Chinese have always organised themselves in mutual aid associations to cope with the hazards of history. Certain secret societies, moreover, have harshly exploited this need for protection. Christian relief agencies, in a fraternal spirit, fill the gaps left by the Chinese network and by the inadequacies of local aid. Diocesan and national charitable agencies do their best to respond to the needs which are brought to their attention.

The progress made by a specifically Chinese apostolate arouses the interest of the local authorities, religious as well as civil. Do the Bishops give effective consideration to the reality of Chinese culture? Within the overall framework of their pastoral system, is effective provision made for the special ministry called for by this ethnic minority? As for local governments, anxious to build up the unity and independence of their nation, they regard with suspicion activities likely to encourage cultural particularism. Is there not a danger of political division? The Christians are contending with a problem which in reality affects the whole of the Chinese diaspora. How may their cultural traditions and social customs be reconciled with total integration into the host nation?

4. CULTURAL FIDELITY AND LOCAL INTEGRATION

Where do the essential loyalties of the Chinese of the diaspora lie? Do they belong fully in the countries in which their ancestors settled, in which they themselves were born, whose language they speak and of which they are often citizens? This is no doubt true of the majority of Chinese in Thailand, for example. In other countries, the Chinese may have integrated very little into the local population, especially if they continue to speak their own language and to open their own schools.

The new nations of South-East Asia demand from them total political loyalty. They have to speak the language of the host country, and even adopt a local name and abandon their Chinese one. Wishing to ensure their own security and to prosper in peace, the Chinese bow to these demands. But they know that their attempts at assimilation do not eliminate all dangers. Their recent experience in Indonesia and Vietnam justifies their hesitation. After having imposed Vietnamese citizenship on all Chinese in 1957, the Saigon government later closed certain professions to them. In 1978, the communist régime confiscated their property and allowed a certain number to flee into China, as if they were Chinese nationals.

Having faced these problems of existence for many years, the overseas Chinese have acquired the habit of ensuring their survival by means of their cultural links and their associations. The bonds which unite them are difficult to define in legal or political terms. Whatever the extent of their integration into the local community, they still share certain deep feelings: love for their country of origin and pride in the achievements of the new China; an attachment to the Chinese language, and frustration when they do not know how to read and write it; respect for family relationships, and the obligation for members of the same clan to help each other; concern for the preservation of a moral heritage of human qualities by means of a good education.

This solid cultural basis allows them great freedom to adapt themselves to a very wide range of social and political situations. They belong to all social groups: peasants, workers, fishermen, small traders, doctors, teachers, technicians, entrepreneurs and businessmen. According to a survey carried out in 150 dioceses in about 1955 by the Catholic Central Bureau, 5 per cent of Chinese were rich, 30 per cent comfortably off, 40 per cent had a modest income and 25 per cent earned the minimum living wage. Few Catholics are found among the very rich. They are more numerous in the middle class rather than among the poorest groups. Students and academics occupy an important place. The most deprived families believe that education and knowledge can open all doors. In response to these hopes, the Church has been able to open schools of a high standard. These schools provide an education in citizenship in accordance with governmental directives and cultivate, at the same time, those values which are peculiar to the Chinese personality.

One of the most delicate problems still facing the Chinese is that of their participation in political life. Any action which seeks to protest against an unjust social order immediately leads to their being suspected of plotting revolution. They often have no other choice but a docile conformity. They sometimes have to pay local officials in order to be left in peace. Their social activities cause them to be suspected of being pro-Peking; their attachment to Chinese culture leads to their being suspected of being pro-Taiwan. This is why they often avoid political involvement, devoting all their energies to trade and to technical services.

5. THE SPECIFIC MISSION OF THE CHRISTIANS OF THE DIASPORA

The directions followed by Chinese Christianity are in harmony with the general conditions of the diaspora.

In general, the Christian faith is a factor which encourages integration into the local community. In public worship and in meetings of Catholic associations, the local language is normally used. On such occasions, the Chinese intermingle with members of the local community. They thus help to open up their own community to other people, other realities. This witness which they offer can at times be costly. It may be that they are rejected by those of their own race, as if baptism meant that they have sold out to the foreigners. This failure of understanding is very painful to them. Not only do these Christians intend to maintain their solidarity with their people, but they also remain attached to those values which belong specifically to their people, and indeed desire to foster them.

In these conditions, the development of a specifically Chinese apostolate could only be greeted with joy. In November 1958 the Office of the Apostolic Visitor issued a note concerning the recent instructions of the Office of Propaganda on the subject of the Chinese rites. The unease created by the interdicts of the past was dispelled. Catholics were allowed to demonstrate fully their loyalty to the tradition of their family. Moreover they are contributing actively to the encouragement of a flourishing family life within the context of modern society. The provisions of Vatican II allow, in addition, the elaboration of a Chinese-language liturgy. Although this is difficult where there are Sunday masses which are open to all the faithful in the locality, celebrations in Chinese are, however, easily performed in small groups. These groups also have the advantage of enabling contacts between the members to take place more easily, thus helping the faith to find expression in a Chinese way. Formerly thought of as a mission field, the Chinese diaspora is gradually becoming aware that it has its own mission as part of the proclamation of the Gospel to the world.

Mgr Van Melckebeke having resigned, exhausted by long years of labour, the Congregation for the Evangelization of the Nations appointed a successor in the person of Mgr Pierre Chung Wan-ting, Archbishop of Kuching in Malaysia, on September 26, 1977. The instructions which he received on that occasion made it clear that 'without creating a church within a church, the various groups of ethnic Chinese must be helped to find a place within the local churches whilst still preserving their identity and their characteristic features'.

A Chinese expression of the Christian life in the world is all the more desirable today since new possibilities of communication between China and the rest of the world are opening up. Since the end of 1977, overseas Chinese can easily spend time in the People's Republic, bringing their technical qualifications and their capital to assist in the development of that country. Christians should readily understand all the human impli-

cations of these new possibilities of interchange. Helping China to overcome its old isolation by their familiarity with international life, they are
also particularly well placed to reveal to the world the ethical and cultural
values of Chinese civilisation.

Translated by Lawrence Ginn

Joseph Spae

Theological China-research since Båstad-Leuven

THE 1974 Båstad-Leuven Conferences (B.-L.) were nothing short of seminal events. They marked the end of a long period of ecclesiastical self-satsfaction. They helped the churches to discover that it was not only hopeless poverty which pushed China into the communist embrace but also their own ineptitude and divisions. The variety and depth of post-B.-L. China-research involves even more decision-makers, sinologists and theologians. It rightly claims a double distinction: it is strongly inter-disciplinary, and strongly ecumenical. Since B.-L., five major conferences were held in 1975, eight in 1976, four in 1977, and two in 1978. Four meetings with considerable promise have been announced for 1979.

1. THE 'SPRING AND AUTUMN ANNALS' OF 1978 BRING FASCINATING NEWS

Theology feeds on events and on the Bible. The Fifth National People's Congress, Peking, February 28-March 5, 1978, dropped a bagful of intriguing happenings on the heads of China-watchers. At this 'Requiem Mass for Mao' Buddhist, Muslim and Christian leaders reappeared as if by magic. This summer, during an extensive trip, six Catholic bishops and thirty priests were interviewed. The Catholic University of Leuven was approached with a view to exchanging professors as well as students with the Institute for the Study of World Religions (Buddhism, Christianity, Islam, Taoism), inaugurated at Peking in October. The Communist Party's *People's Daily* editorialised on October 30 that 'the theory of genius' which deified Mao's thought, 'is the largest ideological obstacle to

China's economic development'. The *Little Red Book* which came out in thirty-six languages and nearly 1,000 million copies is now discredited: 'It dismembers Mao's thought and reduces it to maxims without inner consistency nor proper historical context.' The mighty Teng Hsiao-p'ing recently said: 'If people work hard, the government doesn't care which religion they practise.' China's 950 million people are marching on in a current of fresh air. Theologians stay alert in the reviewing stand!

2. LET A HUNDRED (THEOLOGICAL) FLOWERS BLOOM

What stands out at the theological China-conferences is a common and anguished search for truth and charity towards the Chinese people and the church. Some participants would like 'to change the church so she may be worthy of the new China', a phrase first heard at Leuven. Others see China as a starting point: What is her theological significance, and what challenge does the PCR hold out for the local and the worldwide church? All theologians interrelate both concerns.

To take an elementary look at post-B.-L. developments three meetings are singled out: Columbus (Lutheran), Brugge (Catholic) and Notre Dame (ecumenical).

Columbus, Ohio, May 26-29, 1975. Twelve Lutheran World Federation leaders met, as Arne Sovik writes, 'not to criticise what has been done at Båstad and Leuven, but rather to build on the work done there using resources of our own theological heritage'. In fact, 'Columbus' here stands for a congeries of opinions, generally Lutheran and German Evangelical, related to B.-L., starting with a resounding 'Nein' by Gustave Weth, and followed by a number of statements aptly summarised in the LWF's *Information Letter*, No. 15, August 1976, from which we quote twelve critical remarks and questions addressed to B.-L.:

1. The provisional state of the B.-L. findings was underrated. 2. Leuven and Columbus ignored the problematic of the relationship between religion and revelation, Gospel and ideology. 3. A full and critical evaluation of missionary data was wanting. 4. Notwithstanding the unreliability of our China information bold assertions were made. 5. Theologians with personal experience of an ideology functioning as a quasi-religion were not heard. 6. Recent China events cannot simply be seen as 'the fruits of the Spirit'. 7. 'Participation in God's redemptive activity in and with the world', and 'The full integration of faith and good works,' these remain open questions. 8. We are unclear about the nature and possibilities of natural man. 9. What to think of a power structure that binds people and violates human rights through a con-

tinuing revolution? 10. Can the Westernising of China through Marxism become a preparation for lasting contact with the Church? 11. To what extent must the suffering of Christians in China be attributed not to religious but to political causes? 12. Does comparison with other communist states impose itself?

A final answer to these important questions is still in the making, but a start was made at Brugge.

Brugge, Belgium, October 1-3, 1976. This third meeting of 'Catholics in Europe concerned with China' (CECC) broke new ground by confronting China-watchers with outstanding European theologians, such as Claude Geffré, Domenico Grasso, Luigi Sartori, Jacques Sommet and Hans Waldenfels, who was asked to respond to the 'Columbus' reflections which he did in a five-page paper here summarised:

> Waldenfels agrees with the Columbus points 1, 4 and 11. He asks for more hesitancy in making political and theological judgments. (5) The ecumenical approach depends upon theological stances about which participants should be clear. (2) The possibilities of natural man and the nature of 'transcendental experiences' in China require deeper study. (8) The same must be said about 'the fruits of the Spirit' and 'the full integration of faith and good works'. (6 and 7)

Brugge retained for further study eight important questions:

> 1. In the encounter between Christianity and China, to what extent can orthopraxis (Christianity 'as a way') be stressed over against explicit concern for orthodoxy? 2. What is the relationship between individual and collective conscience and morality? 3. Is China indeed 'a sign of the times'? 4. Which are signs of the Kingdom of God in China? 5. Can one be a Taoist, Confucianist, Maoist, and a Christian at the same time? 6. What is new about the Gospel in regard to China old and new? 7. Is there a common ground between 'to serve the people' and Christian kenosis? 8. What kind of kenotic attitude is called for from the Church in regard to China?

These questions did indeed come up for further study at the CECC meetings in Paris, October 28-30, 1977 (questions 5 and 7) and in Rome, September 28-30, 1978 (questions 1 and 2). And they were very much in evidence at Notre Dame.

Notre Dame, Indiana, June 29-July 2, 1977. The thirty-eight scholars who gathered at the University of Notre Dame came from the synoptic realms of history, philosophy, political science, religion and theology. Notre Dame, in many ways, sharpened the Brugge questions. It even went beyond them in its study of the relation between Christianity and non-Western cultures with a view to a rewording and reliving of theology in a milieu such as that of China. It queried about the hermeneutics of China-events in the face of our monumental ignorance.

Two attitudes stood out: 1. An active listening stance, making the participants anxious to meditate on the Christian self-understanding and on the many hints of the Spirit at work in China. This stance set them free from all defensiveness having little to say on missionary strategy. 2. An introspective mood which led to the recognition of the need for Christian kenosis, that 'emptiness' which is reminiscent of the Buddhist *k'ung* and the Taoist *hsü*: 'This points to an emptying of our missionary agendas and theological presuppositions. In such a self-emptying we might come to hear the word spoken in history. Out of such disciplined hearing may come the selfless witness of the Gospel, be it in China or elsewhere.' (James Whitehead, Introduction to the Notre Dame Proceedings, in press).

3. DEVELOPING THE CHURCHES' CONSCIENCES

B.-L. launched a movement which puts China ever higher on the agenda of Christian churches. China-watchers such as Parig Digan and Jonas Jonson (the Castor and Pollux of B.-L.), Arne Sovik of the LWF, Donald MacInnis and Franklin Woo of the USA, Léon Trivière, Jean Charbonnier and René Laurentin of France, Victor Hayward of England, Bernward Willeke of Germany, Angelo Lazzarotto of Italy, as well as Julia Ching and Michael Chu of China, to mention only a dozen names, have done yeoman's work. Some Bishops' Conferences, such as that of France, have a China dossier for their information. More important perhaps are sets of popular writings for wide distribution throughout the churches, particularly in North America where 'Contemporary China' is an International Education for Mission theme in 1978-79.

Considerable interest also goes to the missionary implications of Christianity's past and present attitudes towards China. It is commonly agreed that the divisions under which Christianity stands racked and riddled share responsibility for the misfortunes which befell the Church in China. B.-L. not only showed that Christian unity for a renewed approach to China is imperative, but later conferences convincingly proved how much we ought and could already do together. We simply have no right to re-export our divisions and burden China as we have done in the past. It is gratifying to report that, to the theologians engaged in China-study, this great nation is seen as an ecumenical challenge of the first magnitude which they intend to meet.

Parig Digan

Centres of Research on the Encounter between Christianity and China

BY AN irony of history, centres of research on the encounter between Christianity and China are a phenomenon largely peculiar to the latest period of *non*-encounter between them. It has been only after the latest closing of the door of China in the face of the Christian world—that is, only after 1949—that interested Christians, deprived of an outlet for their interest in the form of missionary action, have been forced to discover the benefits of standing back and getting the whole picture of their encounter or non-encounter into some sort of perspective. This had not been done in any organised way before. The work of cultural research had scarcely had a separate identity even within the missionary congregations and mission boards, though some impetus was given to this under the auspices of the main Catholic and Protestant co-ordinating bodies, the Congregation for the Propagation of the Faith (dating from 1622) and the International Missionary Council (formed in 1921).

Even within the period since 1949, centres of Christian inspiration concentrating on the study of China were rare and isolated up to the 1970s. The most notable older examples are the China Program of the National Council of Churches (NCC-USA) in New York, the office of *China News Analysis* in Hong Kong, and the Christian Study Centre for Chinese Religion and Culture, also Hong Kong.

The NCC-USA was a leader in the movement to transcend the cold-war relationship between the People's Republic of China and the USA. Besides sponsoring or co-sponsoring many consultations on China, it has published continuously since 1947 a periodical successively called *China*

Bulletin and *China Notes*. The files of this publication are now a major source of documentation on events and ideas of Christian concern relating to contemporary China. At least, they are a source on those events and ideas that have been found compatible with the NCC's commitment to a conciliatory line. For the more unfavourable side of the picture, it has usually been necessary to look elsewhere, at least in the period of the Cultural Revolution. In the eyes of many ex-China missionaries and others, the most authoritative source of critical material on all aspects of the PRC since 1953 has been *China News Analysis*, the product of a quarter-century of monitoring and interpreting by a Hungarian Jesuit, himself an ex-China missionary, Ladislao La Dany. Though the fate of Christianity is only one of many topics in this periodical, an observer of contemporary Christian research on China would get a very good idea of the polarisation of opinion, and indeed of the conflicting character of the available evidence, from a regular perusal of the materials published by these two centres. As for the Christian Study Centre at Tao Fong Shan, Hong Kong, it too has published a periodical, *Ching Feng*. Dating from 1957, it was concerned originally more with the religion and culture of traditional China, but in recent years it has given more space to the contemporary form of the question of Christianity's relations with China. In the search for a suitable focus of international and ecumenical Christian concern with China, the Christian Study Centre has recently been more in view than any other particular location.

It took more than another decade before these three China-study centres ceased to be isolated phenomena; but the change was comparatively dramatic when it came. A survey made by Jonathan Chao in 1976 counted twenty-five Christian China-study centres then existing, and nearly two-thirds of these had been started since the Cultural Revolution (i.e., since 1965). In fact, of the ones there is space to mention here, none has much of a history before 1972. By that year there existed three more undertakings which have since been central to the new currents of interest in the encounter: the Marxism and China Study of the Lutheran World Federation in Geneva, the activities related to contemporary China in the international Catholic research centre Pro Mundi Vita, and the China Study Project, representing a variety of British religious traditions brought together in London. In the same year (1972) in which they learned of each other's existence, these three, together with the NCC China Program in New York, were already forming the links that constituted the early basis of what came to be called the Ecumenical China Study Liaison Group.

In the history of this liaison the crucial year was 1974, when the LWF and PMV jointly sponsored international conferences on China in Bàstad, Sweden, and in Leuven, Belgium. Largely under that impetus, the later 1970s saw a score of notable Christian conferences on China, stimulating new or renewed activity on the part of more than a dozen centres or foci of Christian study of China. Among such centres active in this period, the following are particularly notable: the Canada China Programme of the Canadian Council of Churches in Toronto; the Jesuit China Studies Delegation, hitherto based in New York; the Midwest China Study Resource Center in St Paul, Minnesota; the Methodist China Liaison Office in Hong Kong; the Institute for Chinese studies of the Urban University in Rome; and an evangelical undertaking in Hong Kong, now to be known as the Chinese Church Research Center, directed since 1977 by Jonathan Chao. Other Christian centres which include China as a significant *part* of their studies include Echange France-Asie in Paris, the Institute of Asian Studies in Milan, the Bureau of Asian Affairs in Manila, the research section of Missio in Aachen, and the Asian Bureau Australia in Melbourne.

In a normal situation of encounter, the above would represent only part (the Christian part) of the activity concerned with studying that encounter. In the actual situation, is there no contribution at all from the non-Christian Chinese side? Yes, there is, or at least there may be. In 1978 an Institute for the Study of World Religions, proposed by Mao before the Cultural Revolution, was reported to be taking shape in Peking. For further details see Parig Digan *The Christian China-watchers* (Brussels 1978); Jonathan Chao *Guidelines towards a Christian Understanding of China* (Hong Kong 1977); René Laurentin *Chine et Christianisme* (Paris 1977) pp. 243-250; and the LWF Marxism and China Study *Information Letter.*

Joseph Spae

A Bibliographical Note:
Six Marginal but Important Books

FOR the non-specialist desirous of background information beyond the strictly theological China literature mentioned in this issue of *Concilium*, here is a brief account of six books which could help him with his Church-and-China evaluation.

1. Ching, Julia *Confucianism and Christianity, A Comparative Study* (Tokyo: Kodansha International 1977). Ching is a professional sinologist born in Shanghai. A major part of her book is a critique of the Confucian heritage, centred upon the problem of man (see Munro below), the good and evil in his 'heart', the human and the cultural 'community'. To the question 'Have Confucians and Christians the same God?' her answer is 'Yes, with differences'. Here is a remarkable effort at intercultural and interreligious dialogue, and an introduction to a China-related contextual theology of interest to the universal Church.

2. Gambert, Ruth *Red and Expert, Education in the People's Republic of China* (New York: Schocken Books 1977). The author widely studied all levels of the Chinese educational process. Her book is crammed with *faits divers* but fails to ask the deeper question: What are the limits of remoulding human relations, such as marriage and parenthood, in the light of Mao's theory on social classes? The Chinese cultural climate will not turn favourably to liberal reforms as long as politics and ideology are in command. Meanwhile we applaud the fact that educational facilities have been extended to the masses, thus permitting them, as Mao had hoped, to participate more efficiently in the national regeneration.

3. Lacy, Creighton *Coming Home—to China* (Philadelphia: The Westminster Press 1978). Born in Old China from missionary parents, Lacy's travelogue of 1977 compares the present with the past, which he

finds wanting. By implication he raises important questions such as this: 'Is Maoism an adequate religion for contemporary China?' His upsetting answer: 'Countless sincere followers of Jesus, in the West as well as within China, believe that the social and economic achievements of the PCR come nearer to fulfilling the Magnificat, the Sermon on the Mount, or Jesus' inaugural at Nazareth, than do most so-called Christian societies.' Lacy feels that, for the last thirty years, Mao's revolution was beneficial and that, for the next thirty years, the new programme offers promise that world powers should support but never dominate. His book will contribute to missionary reflection, without, however, bringing relief to theologians anguished by the ambiguity of his observations.

4. Munro, Donald J. *The Concept of Man in Contemporary China* (Ann Arbor: The University of Michigan Press 1977). The book which should be read with the author's *The Concept of Man in Early China* (Stanford University Press 1969), evaluates the different assumptions under which the Confucian and Marxist (both Russian and Chinese) politico-cultural systems operate and even could co-operate. Munro reveals the existence of a number of enduring traits of human behaviour. He comes to the conclusion that Maoism is not all that new. In the Chinese context it cannot but be little interested in 'human rights' as seen by the West. Education is a powerful agent for the transforming of man because, as both Confucius and Mao emphatically assert, he is above all a social being. Munro's books are also a fine introduction to a rethinking of old Western dualisms, such as the body-soul dichotomy; to a re-evaluation of the affective versus the cognitive, of individual versus communal freedom, of man-for-others versus man-for-himself. All these are windows opened by a non-theologian upon crucial theological problems which will always be with us.

5. Terrill, Ross *The Future of China after Mao* (New York: Delta 1978). Here is a quick stock-taking of the post-Mao era mixed with a good deal of futurology on Chinese leadership. Terrill feels that 'the change in the post-Mao era is unlikely to be swift or dramatic; there will be a great deal of bureaucracy in tomorrow's China, and a great deal of privatism on the part of the Chinese man in the street who knows how to sidestep the messy currents of affairs of state'. He is realistic when he adds that individual freedom as the West knows it is not on the cards for China, and that other values seem more important, such as economic security, pride of the nation, 'and a chance to participate in the cut and thrust of community life'. Maoism may remain, 'but modifications to it will bring important changes in the life of the Chinese people'. Terrill is convinced that Buddhism shall not revive, nor shall Christianity. To which, in all logic, he should have added the final realistic question: Who knows?

6. Wilson, Dick, ed. *Mao Tse-tung in the Scales of History* (Cam-

bridge: Cambridge University Press 1977). Wilson presents ten important papers by scholars specialising in Mao and his time. Here then is a
composite biography brought together shortly after the Great Helms-
man's death in September 1976. The book weighs Mao as philosopher
(truth and action are interwoven; socialism, unlike the industrial revolution, is all about changing human nature; leaders must listen to the led), as
Marxist (Mao abandoned the Marxist notion of history's inexorable
forward march in favour of a certain indeterminacy), as political leader
(the Cultural Revolution is one of his failures), as soldier (Mao still lives
on his reputation but the substance of his originality and renown was lost
in 1949), as teacher (Mao wrestles with the contradiction of communists
as owners of the truth yet in need of help from others), as economist (Mao
said: 'I am a complete outsider when it comes to economic construction'),
as patriot (he hoped to change China's traditions into a revolutionary
stance, based upon the daily travail of the people), and as statesman (he
was not a world statesman and had no interest in becoming one). The
verdict: 'Having supplied China with a new orthodoxy, with a new sense
of international self-respect and with a minimum degree of social change
necessary, Mao was in the end rebuffed.' The final chapter describes Mao
as an innovator. It gives him high marks as a prophet of hope, com-
municating 'the vitality of possibility, the vision of justice'. The acid test
for Mao is this: 'Will China go beyond the mere application of Marxism;
will it stand for a four-square reappraisal of what life is all about?' To this
and similar questions, not the book but history seems in a hurry to suggest
the answer.

Contributors

JEAN CHARBONNIER was born in Paris in 1932 and ordained in 1957 as a priest of the Missions Etrangères de Paris. After obtaining a *licence* in the teaching of philosophy (Sorbonne 1959), he had ten years of extensive experience of pastoral work in Singapore (1960-70), especially in Chinese-speaking communities. After 1970 he taught sacramental anthropology at the Centre d'Etudes Missionaires in Chevilly-la-rue. In 1973 he gained a doctorate in theological sciences from the Institut Catholique de Paris for his thesis on *Identité culturelle et modernisation à Singapour*. After further research in the Far East and in Paris, he completed his *thèse d'état* on *L'interprétation de l'histoire en Chine contemporaine* (Lille 1979). He has also published various articles, and a series of dossiers for the Service d'information des Missions Etrangères de Paris. He visited the People's Republic of China in 1977 and 1978.

HUNG CHIH. For security reasons, the author, known to the editors, publishes this article under a pseudonym.

JULIA CHING, associate professor, Yale University, now visiting professor at the University of Toronto, is a specialist in Eastern religious philosophy. She has published before in *Concilium*.

PARIG DIGAN is Irish and was born in 1929. He is a member of the Missionary Society of St Columba and was ordained a priest in 1953. He has done missionary work in the Philippines as parish priest, college director, etc. from 1956-69. He has been PMV researcher, Asia Section, since 1971. He has written on religion and China, Japan, Indonesia, Philippines, etc.

CLAUDE GEFFRÉ, OP, is professor of fundamental theology and director of doctoral studies in the theology and religious studies section of the Institut Catholique in Paris. He is the author of *Un nouvel âge de la théologie* (Paris 1972) and has contributed to *Procès de l'objectivité de Dieu* (Paris 1969), *Révélation de Dieu et langage des hommes* (Paris 1972), *Herméneutique de la sécularisation* (Paris 1976), *Le déplacement de la théologie* (Paris 1977), *La Révélation* (Brussels 1977).

CLAUDE LARRÉ, a member of the Society of Jesus, was born in 1919. He studied Chinese in Peking and Shanghai (1947-1952), Japanese in Japan and Vietnamese in Saigon. He now teaches in Paris at the Institut Catholique, the Centre Sèvres and the Ecole Européenne d'Acupuncture, and runs the Institute Ricci, the centre for Chinese studies there. He has written articles to open the Western mind to Chinese thought, and his published works include: *Mao et la Vieille Chine, Le Livre de la Voie at de la Vertu* (translation and commentary), and *Structures de l'Acupuncture traditionnelle*.

STANISLAUS LOKUANG was born on January 1, 1911, in the Diocese of Hunan-henyang, on the Chinese mainland. After his ordination in 1936, he stayed in Rome as a professor at the Urban University and a consultant of the Chinese Embassy to the Holy See. In 1961 he was appointed Bishop of Tainan, Taiwan. During the Vatican Council he was a vice-chairman of the commission for the missions. He was named Archbishop of Taipei on February 15, 1966. He is also a member of committees to make a revision of canon law and to contact non-Christian religions and areligious people, and he is the secretary of the commission of Asian Bishops. He is Rector of Fu Jen University. His publications include *Points of Chinese Philosophy* (1975), *Metaphysics of Confucianists* (1959), *A History of Chinese Philosophical Thought* (1975-1978).

DONALD MACINNIS was born in Jefferson, Wisconsin and was ordained in the New York East Conference of the Methodist Church in June 1953. Mr MacInnis was appointed a Methodist missionary in 1948. He was a district superintendent of the Taiwan Provisional Annual Conference, 1959-65, and lecturer at Taiwan Theological College and Soochow University. He is a member of the National Committee on U.S.-China Relations, the China Council of the Asia Society and the Association of Asian Studies. His publications include *Religious Policy and Practice in Communist China: a Documentary History* (New York 1972) and numerous articles in *Christian Century* and other journals.

MICHEL MASSON, SJ, was born in Paris in 1937. He studied sinology in Taiwan, then at Harvard where he specialised in the history and thought of modern China. He belongs to the Jesuit Centre d'Etudes et de

Recherches in Paris ('Centre Sèvres') and at present lives in Hong Kong where he is continuing his research on the intellectual movements in China from 1930 onwards.

LUIGI SARTORI was born in Roanna (Vicenza) in 1924 and was ordained in 1946. He taught philosophy at the Seminary of Padua and at present holds the chair of theology there. He also teaches theology in the Faculty of Theology in Milan. He has edited the theological journal *Studia Patavina*, and has also contributed to other journals. He is a member of the 'Faith and Constitution' section of the Ecumenical Council of Churches. As well as many art articles and essays he has published: *Blondel ed il cristianesimo* (Padua 1953); *Teologia della storia* (Padua 1956); *E Dio il regista della storia?* (Milan 1961).

YU-MING SHAW is a Chinese by birth who lived on the Chinese mainland and in Taiwan from 1938 to 1965. He is Assistant Professor of History, University of Notre Dame, Notre Dame, Indiana, USA, and Associate, Center for Far Eastern Studies, the University of Chicago. He is author of chapters in several books and of articles in many scholarly journals, and co-editor of a forthcoming book on China and the West *The Religious Dimension*.

JOSEPH SPAE was born at Lochristi, Belgium, in 1913. He studied orientalism and Buddhism at Leuven, Peking, Kyoto (Otani and Imperial University), and Columbia University, New York, where he obtained a doctorate in Far Eastern languages and philosophy. In 1961 he founded the Oriens Institute for Religious Research in Tokyo. In 1972-1976 he served as Secretary General of Sodepax in Rome and Geneva. At present he is Consulter of the Vatican Secretariat for Non-Christians and Co-director (with Robert Schreiter) of the Chicago Institute for Theology and Culture, established in 1978, with special responsibility for Asia and Europe. His books include *Christianity Encounters Japan* (Tokyo 1968), *Japanese Religiosity* (Tokyo 1971), *Shinto Man* (Tokyo 1972), *Buddhist-Christian Empathy* (in preparation).

EDMOND TANG was born in Hong Kong in 1947, studied philosophy at the University of Hong Kong and theology at the Katholieke Universiteit te Leuven (Belgium). He was a staff member of the Hong Kong Centre for Pastoral Studies from 1974-5 and lecturer at the Holy Spirit Seminary from 1975-6. Since 1977 he has been on the research staff at Pro Mundi Vita, an international research and information centre in Brussels.

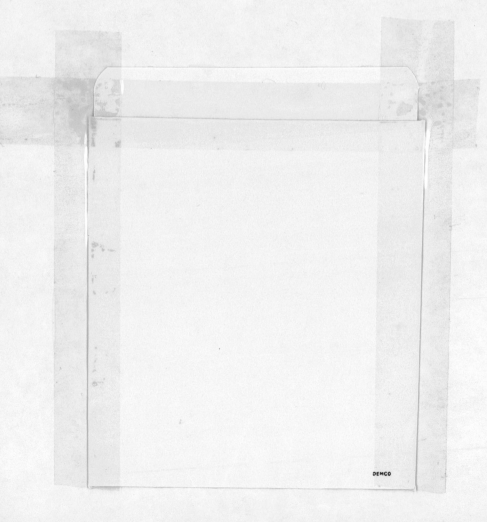

DEMCO